Bright Ide[...]
Teacher
Handbooks
Language
Resources

Publisher's note
A cassette and booklet of Singing and
dancing games using many of the songs
included in this book is available from the
publishers.

Price £5.00

Published by Scholastic Publications Ltd,
Marlborough House, Holly Walk,
Leamington Spa, Warwickshire CV32 4LS

© 1987 Scholastic Publications Ltd
Reprinted 1987

Contributors: Leonora Davies,
Frankie Leibe, Julia Matthews.
Edited by Priscilla Chambers
Designed by Dave Cox
Sub-edited Jackie Cunningham-Craig and
Annette Heuser
Photographs by Dave Richardson

Printed in Great Britain by Ebenezer Baylis,
Worcester

ISBN 0 590 70692 6

Front and back covers: photograph by Martyn
Chillmaid; Children's clothes courtesy of Mothercare.

Contents

Contents

Introduction

As parents and as teachers we are delighted by the language development of our children, from their early cooing and babbling, through first words and on to whole sentences. At each stage we are challenged by their desire to make themselves understood, their desire to communicate with other people. A significant step along the way is the constant play with language in which young children indulge. They play with the sounds of language from an early age and delight proud parents with their repeated syllables 'da-da-da' and 'ma-ma-ma'.

Frequently, when they are on their own, young children take the opportunity to further their own language development. They try out newly acquired words and repeat them over and over again in order to hear the sounds and fix the patterns in their mind. They often sing phrases and ritualise these routines in their solitary play. This sort of activity flourishes in an environment where language is used for a wide range of purposes. The environment, in turn, gives children a rich and stimulating language experience on which to draw.

Children use language to regulate their own actions and influence the actions of others. They use language to solve problems and to work things out. From this point of view the importance and significance of language in education is well known to us all and cannot be stressed enough. However, there is the argument, expressed by some research findings, that language development is complete before children enter school. Clearly an enormous amount of language development has taken place during the pre-school years, but this should not deny the fact that children's language is bound to continue to grow – to be added to, elaborated upon, refined, re-applied and re-organised in the years ahead. Indeed adapting, creating and using language is the key to further learning.

Language as an object

One of the most important phases of development which takes place during the school years is the child's growing ability to use language as an object in its own right and to use language to act upon itself. This dramatic cognitive change, some argue, is an essential ingredient for successful literacy learning. For instance, children with reading difficulties have been found to be remarkably insensitive to rhyme and alliteration.

This shift in understanding enables the child to reflect on language, to play with it and to use it to make desired effects. It gives them greater control over their linguistic repertoire and enables them to become more skilful in their own use of language. Poetry writing or appreciation, for instance, would be impossible without this skill.

This ability to use language as an object in its own right becomes particularly apparent when we observe children writing. They read through what they have written to check that it sounds right; sometimes they alter a word, or add or edit out parts they wish to change. Skill in these activities continues to develop throughout the school years and beyond.

Here we see an example of the relationship between talking, listening, reading and writing. This relationship can easily be lost when we think about the curriculum for primary-aged children. It is our responsibility as teachers to take care to forge as many links as possible between spoken and written language – using talking and listening to foster reading and writing, as well as using written language (read aloud) as a stimulus for oral work.

Using language games

Language games are an essential ingredient of the reflexive process which helps children to continue playing with language for its own sake and to keep learning about language and the way it works. Nursery rhymes, singing games with matching actions and rhythms of all kinds help to make language easier to recall and reproduce. These activities formalise the language in use and offer opportunities for language play to occur.

The ability to use language reflexively is easily identified in young children when it occurs. At one moment, all jokes, for instance, are lost on young children. And then, all of a sudden they get the trick. At first they get the general idea of a 'punch line' but get it wrong every time. Gradually, as they become more sensitive to langauge ambiguity, they quickly move into a phase of puns and word jokes which are usually preceded by peals of laughter even before the joke is shared.

How we can help

As always in education, developmental processes cannot be left to emerge. As teachers we are continually shaping and facilitating the progress of our children, particularly in the sphere of language development. The games and activities in this book are examples of those language learning contexts we are frequently seeking. We are constantly looking for a wealth of engaging and enriching moments which will lead children on towards making their own discoveries about the way language works. These activities provide motivating structures within which our children's language learning can flourish. They are also deeply embedded in our cultural heritage.

This collection of language activities includes well-known and loved rhymes, games, songs, poems and jokes, not only all the favourite ones from our own childhood but also new ones as well. It is a rich resource for the busy classroom teacher and a welcome addition to any staff-room shelf.

Each activity has clearly written objectives and an indication is given of the age group of children who would benefit most. Inevitably, there are implications for classroom organisation which are associated with some of the activities in this book and in each case the contributor has given helpful information to achieve the best results. Also, there are many ideas for follow-up work and ways of integrating each activity into other work in the classroom. These sections provide an invaluable source of reference for the busy teacher and will provide great pleasure both for you and for the children you teach.

Dr Bridie Raban
University of Reading
School of Education

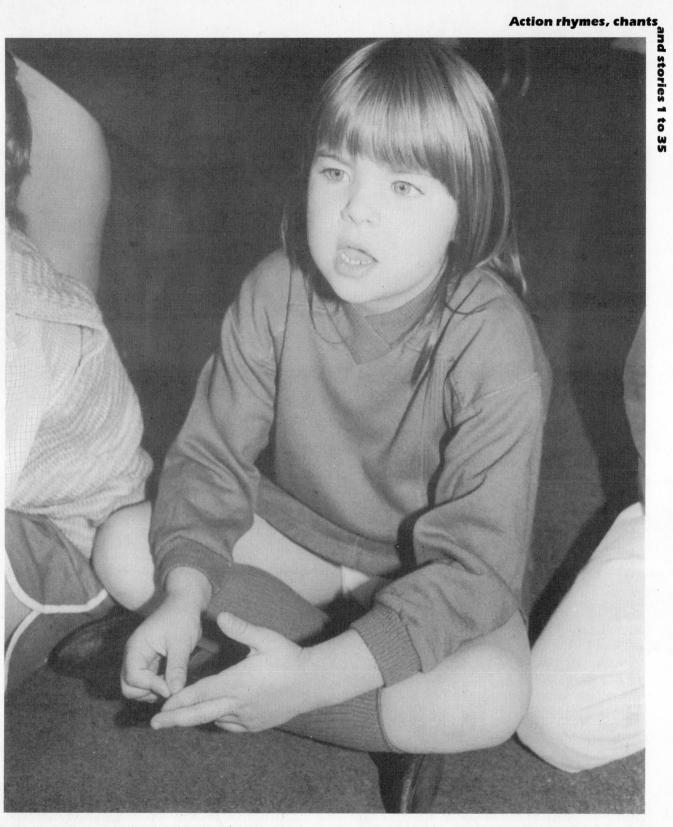

Action rhymes, chants and stories

Action rhymes, chants and stories

INTRODUCTION

Leonora Davies has had many years of teaching experience at all levels of education from infants to higher education. She is presently music co-ordinator with the ILEA; working alongside teachers in the classroom, setting up in-service activities and generally co-ordinating music-making events. Her publications include *Sound Waves* published by Bell & Hyman and the *Primary Music Course* published by Oxford University Press. She is a frequent contributor of both articles and songs to *Child* and *Junior Education* and has also produced and compiled many resource cassettes for Scholastic Publications.

Action rhymes offer many young children their first opportunity for corporate participation and response. As well as the important contribution they make to children's linguistic and physical development they also provide vital opportunities for developing children's social and communication skills.

Although action rhymes are traditionally associated with younger children, some of the ideas presented here have been adapted and developed to span the entire primary age range. The combination of rhythmic movements and the patterning and repetition of the language in action rhymes provides the basis for a number of important learning skills. Finger play rhymes, in particular,

with the combination of rhythmic repetitious use of language, as in 'Miss Polly had a dolly' and simple descriptive movements as in 'Incy wincy spider' help to provide children with early learning experiences which are fundamental to further linguistic and physical growth.

Many of the movement rhymes and chants have a creative structure which provides suitable opportunities for freely adapting, or building onto existing material or creating new material based on an original idea. Adapting, creating and using language provides a key to most further learning situations. Motivation to use language is an important part of creative play and encourages children to explore and discover so much for themselves. The

2

material in this chapter offers opportunities for children to build on these natural capacities.

About the material

The material in this chapter has been divided into six main categories: for the very young; finger play; movement rhymes and songs; chants and songs; and action story songs.

Many of the rhymes and songs give children scope to 'locate' them in their own environment or adapt them to make them more immediately accessible. 'As I walked up to . . .' invites children to insert a geographical location that means something to them. 'The wheels on the bus' and 'The farmer' are structured in such a way as to invite children to make up and to insert suitable verses of their own. These are all important processes in children's learning how to use and to extend language.

The co-ordination of both language and movement can, initially, be a little overwhelming for very young children. Many will respond at first by joining in with the movements alone and only gradually acquire the necessary co-ordination to combine these with the words. Finger play rhymes provide a secure and often sedentary opportunity for allowing these

skills to develop and for children to acquire the necessary confidence needed before they move around in a larger space and use bigger body movements.

Presenting and introducing the material

One very significant factor when presenting these rhymes and songs to the children is the choice of speed at which they are sung or recited. This is particularly important if we are to help children to acquire and to develop skills and confidences. The finger play rhymes need to be introduced initially quite slowly so that the children can enjoy the movements to the full and then begin to co-ordinate them with the speech patterns. Teachers need to observe the children carefully and be aware of individual children's stages of development. It is quite likely that a child's language skills may be at a different stage of development to their physical and co-ordination skills. As children acquire these confidences and skills you can introduce reciting the same rhyme at different speeds. This will help to reinforce the 'musical' idea of *fast and slow* and where appropriate the idea of getting

At first children might find it a little difficult to combine the words with the movements.

faster and slower.

Different moods can be introduced in the same way with even the simplest of material. Invite the children to choose 'how' to say a rhyme ie 'happy', 'sad', 'cross' etc. This will add another interesting dimension to say a rhyme, ie 'happy', 'sad', 'cross' etc. chants are constructed in such a way that they produce their own natural meter, eg 'I can hear my hands go . . .' and 'I'm a little tea pot'. These provide children with early rhythmic experiences, though not all the rhymes and poems need to be chanted in this exacting way and children must be encouraged to experiment and to speak the verses quite freely and away from the strict meter.

Significant pauses can be built into some of the verses to provide added interest. Children love the anticipation which ensues when this happens.

The songs and rhymes selected for this chapter have very simple repetitive melodies and should be sung unaccompanied at a pitch appropriate to both teacher and pupil. None of this 'music' material requires any specialist knowledge, apart from mastering the tune. Class teachers, with their close and intimate knowledge of their own children are the most suitable and appropriate people to share and to enjoy all this material with their class.

As Barbara Tizard and Martin Hughes said in their book, *Young Children Learning*: 'Word games are a great source of pleasure, but they also have educational value. An important part of becoming literate is the ability to see words as objects which can be reflected upon and manipulated. One route to acquiring this ability is through games like these, in which the child plays with words rather than toys.'

For the very young 1

Objectives

To give very young children some ideas and stimulus for early basic movement experiences. All the verses selected suggest some movement qualities and will help children to develop basic co-ordination skills.

Level of development

Three- to five-year-olds.

Classroom organisation

To introduce the verses to the children, recite them slowly. This will give the children time to interpret the movement suggestions. Encourage them to respond to the suggested qualities.

Isolate one or two particular movements, such as hopping, whirling or different ways of walking. Allow children to 'practise' these quite freely before interpreting them again within the context of the verses. The verses could also be used as 'straight' poems, to enjoy on the carpet as part of quiet or story time.

Whisky frisky

Whisky frisky,
Hippity-hop!
Up he goes
To the tree top!

Whirly, twirly,
Round and round,
Down he scampers
To the ground.

Furly, curly
What a tail!
Tall as a feather,
Broad as a sail!

Where's his supper?
In the shell;
Snappy, cracky,
Out it fell.

So silently

As soft as feathers,
As quiet as can be,
Something is falling
So silently.

As white as daisies,
Down from the skies
Something is flying
Like butterflies.

As soft as feathers
It floats to the ground:
Snowflakes are falling
Without a sound.

Hilda I. Rostron

Up and down

Nod your head,
Bend you knees,
Grow as tall as Christmas trees.

On your knees
Slowly fall,
Curl yourself into a ball.

Raise your head,
Jump up high,
Wave your hand and say 'Goodbye'.

G. O. Cross

Where my feet go

In Autumn I scuffled in golden leaves,
In Winter I walked on white snow;
In Spring I tiptoed through new green grass
To places where snowdrops grow.

But now it is Summer, my feet have fun;
They're running to greet the sea.
I splash on gold sand in the dancing waves
And the tide comes up to meet me.

Hilda I. Rostron

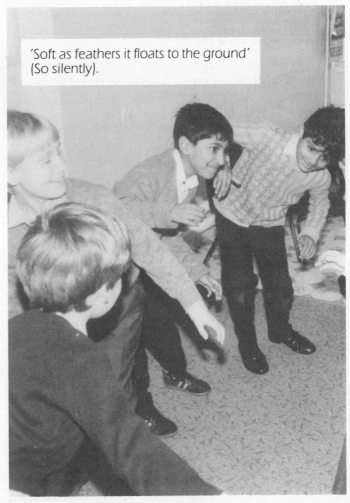

'Soft as feathers it floats to the ground' (So silently).

For the very young 2

Objectives

The following four verses focus on specific rhythmic movements. Once the children are familiar with them you will be able to introduce the idea of altering the speed at which they are said.

Level of development

Three- to five-year-olds.

Classroom organisation

Children will find it easy to join in with these verses because of the underlying rhythmic elements.

In the fun boat

Rocking, rocking,
Here we go!
Rocking, rocking,
To and fro.
I pull – you pull;
Oh, what fun!
Rocking, rocking,
In the sun.

Children sit opposite each other in pairs and rock backwards and forwards marking the pulse beat as they move. When the children are familiar with the words and the movement try lengthening the meter on 'I pull – you pull' then resume the original pulse.

A skipping rhyme

Over our heads
And under our toes,
Round and round
The skipping-rope goes,
Over our heads
And under our toes,
If we are nimble,
The skipping-rope goes.

Let the children jump, keeping the pulse, as they recite. Initially keep the speed fairly slow. As the children acquire greater co-ordination try the verses at differing speeds. Let the children try out different ways of jumping and keeping the beat – both feet together, or one foot and then the other. (Very young children often find it quite difficult to jump with both feet together.)

I'm a little teapot

An 'old' favourite which speaks for itself.

I'm a little teapot, short and stout,
(*Make yourself stout*)
Here's my handle,
(*One arm on waist*)
Here's my spout
(*Hold out the other like a spout*)
When I get my steam up
(*Start to bounce up and down*)
Hear me shout
Tip me up and pour me out!
(*Let the children really enjoy the last line.*)

I wiggle my fingers

A freely spoken rhyme that may help
children to quiet down and 'feel' still.
(Could be useful on a number of occasions.)

I wiggle my fingers
(*Do this then pause*)
I wiggle my toes
(*Pause*)
I wiggle my elbows
(*Pause*)
I wiggle my nose
(*Pause*)
No more wiggles left in me
(*Gradually slow down*)
I'm still . . . as still . . . as still . . . as . . . can . . . be.

Finger play 1

Objectives

Finger play rhymes provide ideal material
for helping to develop and build up young
children's confidence and sense of security.

Level of development

Four- to five-year-olds.

Classroom organisation

These verses can be shared with a whole
class but a more intimate atmosphere can be
created with a small group in the quiet area.
This closer sense of communication
between all the participants is a valuable
and significant factor in helping to build
children's confidence. It also means that you
can be more aware and make closer
observations of individual children.

Children need to be able to join in at
their own level and to begin with many
children may participate with the
movements only.

Initially you will need to take the major
role in speaking the verses. The timing of
this is very important. Allow the children
enough time to co-ordinate the movements.
Repeat verses more than once. Children

enjoy the security of repetition. A number of fundamental skills are 'practised' in repeating the same thing over and over again. As the children become familiar with the rhymes introduce the idea of saying them at different speeds.

A finger play

Close your fingers,
Open them wide,
Make a nest and peep inside.

Open your fingers,
Make them clap,
Lay your hands low in your lap.

Flutter your fingers
To the sky;
Give them wings like birds that fly.

Dance your fingers
Round and round –
Autumn leaves fall to the ground.

Open your fingers
Through them peep,
Fold them now, sing them to sleep.

(Sing a favourite bedtime lullaby)

Hilda I. Rostron

Getting up

Five baby crocuses,
Each a sleepy head;
(Left hand tightly clenched)
Someone shook their blanket
And sang: 'Get out of bed!'
(Right hand gently shakes wrist of left hand)

Five baby crocuses
Opened sleepy eyes;
(Half open fingers of left hand)
Someone shook their blanket
And sang: 'It's time to rise!'
(Right hand gently shakes wrist of left hand)

Five tall crocuses,
Wide-eyed in a ring;
(Left hand fingers stand up straight)
Robin sang: 'Good morning,
It's time to meet the Spring.'
(Left hand shakes right hand in greeting)
And they did!
(Clap hands three times)

Hilda I. Rostron

Here are the lady's knives and forks

Here are the lady's knives and forks
(Interweave fingers together standing up)
Here is the lady's table
(Interweave fingers together pointing into the knee to form a 'table' across the knuckles and back of the hand)
Here is the lady's looking glass
(Point index fingers into an inverted 'V' shape)
And here is the baby's cradle.
(Little fingers make the same shape and rock hands)

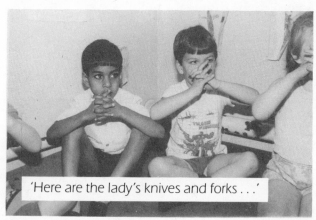

'Here are the lady's knives and forks . . .'

Incy wincy spider

Incy Wincy spider climbed up the spout
(Revolve thumbs and index fingers in a climbing action)
Down came the raindrops and
(Flutter fingers down to knees)
And washed poor Wincy out
(Move flat hands back and fore)
Out came the sunshine
And dried up all the rain
(Palms of hands lift up to make a 'sun' shape)
And Incy Wincy spider climbed up again.
(Repeat the first action)

'Incy wincy spider climbed up the spout'

Tommy Thumb

Tom - my Thumb Tom - my Thumb Where are you?

Here I am Here I am How do you do?

Tommy Thumb

Tommy Thumb, Tommy Thumb where are you?
Here I am. Here I am. How do you do?
(*Wiggle one thumb from behind your back. Wiggle the other from behind your back. Point them together and 'nod' on 'How do you do?'*)

Continue with other fingers as follows:
Verse 2 – Peter Pointer . . . index finger
Verse 3 – Timmy Tall . . . middle finger
Verse 4 – Ruby Ring . . . ring finger
Verse 5 – Sammy Small . . . little finger
Verse 6 – Fingers all.

The rocket

At the rocket launching site
(*Spread both hands wide*)

Stands the rocket, gleaming white
(*Hold up left arm as rocket*)

Here's stage 1, tall and strong
(*Point to forearm*)

Here's stage 2, not so long
(*Point to clenched fist*)

Here's stage 3, not so wide
(*Point to middle finger*)

Here's the module, with the astronauts inside
(*Put right fist clenched, on top of middle finger*)

10, 9, 8, 7, 6, 5, 4, 3, 2, 1, zero
Blast off! and very soon
The module lands upon the moon.
(*The rocket takes off. Left arm falls away, leaving right fist to spread fingers downward, like the legs of the module, and laid slowly on the knee*)

Growing

Flowers grow like this
(*Cup hands like petals opening*)
Trees grow like this
(*Spread arms and fingers*)
I grow
(*Jump up and stretch whole body*)
Just like that!

'Tommy Thumb, Tommy Thumb where are you?'

9

Finger play 2

Objectives

These rhymes invite more specific responses from the children.

Level of development

Five- to seven-year-olds.

Classroom organisation

Use these songs and rhymes to explore ideas of loud and quiet. Experiment with different sounds that can be made with hands and fingers. Sing them at different speeds.

Loud and soft

Clap, clap, clap, clap,
Clap your hands and twist them round.
Tap, tap, tap, tap,
Tap them gently on the ground.

Stamp, stamp, stamp, stamp,
Stamp your feet with all your might.
Tap, tap, tap, tap,
Tap your toes, so soft and light.

Rock, rock, rock, rock,
Now it's time to go to bed.
Hush, hush, hush, hush,
Shut your eyes, you sleepy head.

K. Todd

Everyone can clap hands

Ev - ery one can clap hands clap hands clap hands.
Ev - ery one can clap hands just like me.

I can wiggle my fingers

I can wig-gle my fin-gers I can wig-gle my toes.

I can wig-gle my el-bows I can wig-gle my bones.

I can wig-gle my tum-my I can wig-gle my head. But

Oh I would much rath-er wig-gle my nose in-stead.

Everyone can clap hands

Everyone can clap hands, clap hands, clap hands
Everyone can clap hands just like me.

Go round the group and let everyone who wishes to make up a verse about sounds that their hands and fingers make. Modify the rhythm to fit in the words.

'Everyone can click fingers' or
'Everyone can rub hands/shake fingers' etc . . .

Start by clapping/rubbing/clicking all through the beat. Later clap/rub/click just on the beats indicated.

I can wiggle my fingers

I can wiggle my fingers
I can wiggle my toes
I can wiggle my elbows
I can wiggle my bones
I can wiggle my tummy
I can wiggle my head
But oh I would much rather
Wiggle my nose instead.

K. Baylis

Stand in a circle to do this rhyme so that everyone can see each other. Pause significantly at the end of each phrase and particularly before the last one. Children love the anticipation of this. Make your voice sound really nasal as you 'wiggle' your nose with your fingers.

I can hear my hands go clap, clap, clap

I can hear my hands go clap, clap, clap
I can hear my feet go tap, tap, tap
I can hear my knees go slap, slap, slap
But I can't hear my head go ———.

Try to encourage the children to make the appropriate sounds when they say the appropriate words. This will make the significance of the last line all the more important. Keeping 'silent' beats is an important stage in rhythmic development.

Movement rhymes and songs 1

Objectives

The following three rhymes gently encourage children to use more and bigger scaled movements. Each song introduces a different musical idea.

Level of development

Five- to seven-year-olds.

Classroom organisation

These songs can be introduced in the classroom as a class activity. Use the actions suggested for each song or you (or your class) could make up your own.

Father Abraham

Father Abraham had seven sons
Seven sons had Father Abraham
And they didn't eat
And they didn't sleep
And they had a rotten time.

A nonsense song with fairly silly actions but children love it. Repeat, first swinging one arm, then both arms, then one leg, then arms, leg and head. Start slowly and gradually get quicker. Try it the opposite way, from quick to slow. Which is easier?

Father Abraham

Father A-bra-ham had sev-en sons, Sev-en sons had Fa-ther A-bra-ham, And they did-n't eat, and they did-n't sleep and they had a rot-ten time.

Fly, fly, fly

Fly, fly, fly
Flap your wings and fly.
See how the eagle goes
Flying through the sky.

This is a lovely song for bird movements. Flap your wings three times to the right then three times to the left then move hands all around in the appropriate way. Start the

song slowly, then repeat it faster and faster. Encourage the children to make up verses about other types of birds. 'See how the sparrow goes flying through the sky,' 'See how the robin goes hopping on the path,' 'Still as the flamingo standing on one leg' etc. The song could be introduced as part of a project on birds or on flight.

Fly, fly, fly

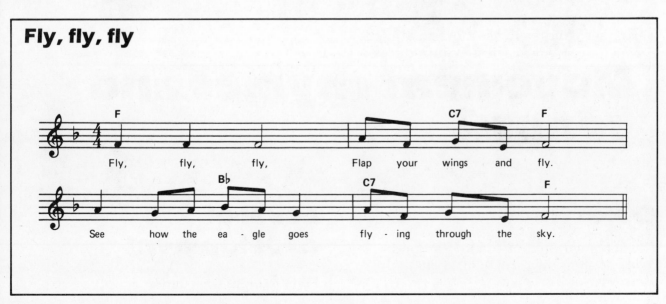

Fly, fly, fly, Flap your wings and fly. See how the ea-gle goes fly-ing through the sky.

Jack-in-the-box

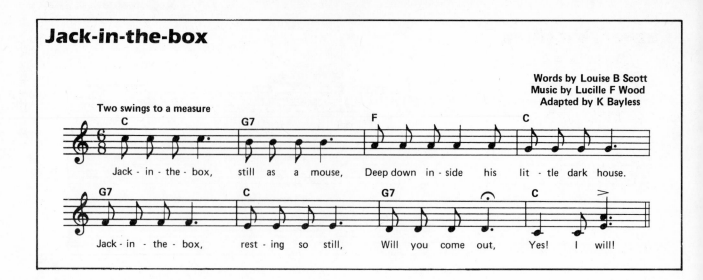

Words by Louise B Scott
Music by Lucille F Wood
Adapted by K Bayless

Two swings to a measure

Jack - in - the - box, still as a mouse, Deep down in - side his lit - tle dark house.

Jack - in - the - box, rest - ing so still, Will you come out, Yes! I will!

Jack-in-the-box

Jack-in-the-box still as a mouse
Deep down inside his little dark house
Jack-in-the box resting so still
Will you come out? Yes! I will!

This song introduces the idea of pitch –

going from high to low then to high again.
Dramatise the idea of stepping into the box,
pulling the lid gradually down, bending
knees further and further at the end of each
phrase. Use the pause to great effect.
Children will enjoy the anticipation before
leaping up at the end.

Movement rhymes and songs 2

Objectives

To encourage children to move around
freely on their own and to make up their
own verses.

Level of development

Five- to eight-year-olds.

14

Classroom organisation

These songs and rhymes can be taught as a class activity. It helps, however, if you can use the hall so that there will be ample room for the children to move freely. Many of the verses can easily be adapted. Encourage the children to try to make up their own words.

The wheels on the bus

The wheels on the bus go round and round
Round and round and round and round
The wheels on the bus go round and round
All day long.

The horn on the bus goes peep, peep, peep . . .
The wipers on the bus go swish, swish, swish . . .
The bell on the bus goes ting, ting, ting . . .

Children do all the actions as they sing. Encourage them to make up verses about the people on the bus:

The mummies on the bus go . . .
The children on the bus make too much noise . . .
The babies on the bus . . .

This song can also be sung about all kinds of vehicles – cars, trains, fire engines, tractors. It can be used as part of a project on transport.

'The wheels on the bus go round and round . . .'

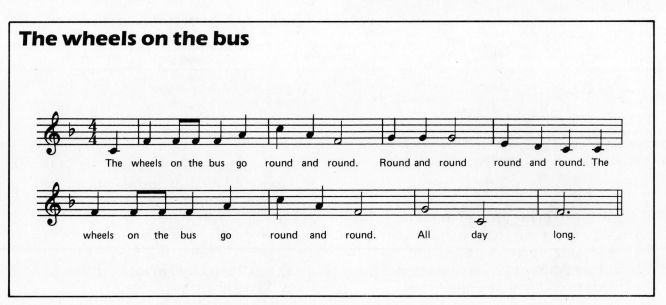

The wheels on the bus

The wheels on the bus go round and round. Round and round round and round. The wheels on the bus go round and round. All day long.

'I can shake my hands like this . . .' (The dingle dangle scarecrow).

The dingle dangle scarecrow

When all the cows were sleeping
And the sun had gone to bed
Up jumped a scarecrow
And this is what he said.

Chorus:
I'm a dingle dangle scarecrow
With a flippy floppy hat
I can shake my hands like this
And shake my feet like that.

Verse 2
When all the hens were roosting
And the moon behind a cloud
Up jumped a scarecrow
And shouted very loud – *Chorus (loud)*

Verse 3
When dogs were in their kennels
And the pigeons in their loft
Up jumped a scarecrow
And whispered very soft – *Chorus (very quietly).*

Crouch down on the ground until the chorus. Leap up and shake hands and feet and head, singing in the 'mood' indicated. The children can get very excited so it is a good idea to end with the quiet verse.

As I walked up to the park one day

As I walked up to the park one day
Park one day, park one day
As I walked up to the park one day
So early in the morning.

This song has infinite possibilities. Encourage the children to move in the way indicated. Vary the speed of the verses accordingly. They can choose where they would like to go, ie skip, run etc. They could sing about what they see at the 'park', the 'station' or the 'market'. They can change the time of day that they go etc.

Tantarra tsing boom

I'm a little one man band
Marching up and down the land
Playing clarinet and flute
Then the fiddle then the lute
Last of all the big bass drum
Tara tara tsing boom
Tantarara tsing boom.

Let the children march all over the hall/playground imitating the playing of the various instruments. (You may like to discuss this with them at some time and show them pictures or the real instruments.) The rhythm of the words for the big bass drum can be chanted in many different ways. Experiment with this.

The dingle dangle scarecrow

When all the cows were sleep-ing and the sun had gone to bed. Up jumped a scare-crow and this is what he said. I'm a din-gle dan-gle scare-crow with a flip-py flop-py hat. I can shake my hands like this And shake my feet like that.

Would you dare?

Would you dare, would you dare
To dance round the room with a big shaggy bear?

Will you try, will you try
To wipe a tear from an elephant's eye?

Would you smile, could you smile
As you sat on the back of a long crocodile?

Would you ever, would you ever
Tickle a lion with a yellow feather?

Will you make, will you make
Friends with a slithering ten foot long snake?

After the children have learned the verse let them work in pairs to devise their own appropriate actions to go with each section. They could take it in turns to mime or dramatise each part. Encourage children to make up their own nonsense verses.

As I walked up to the park one day

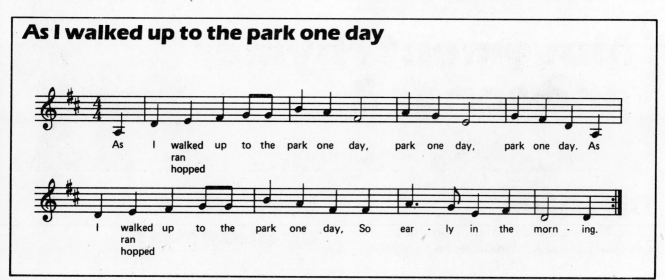

As I walked up to the park one day, park one day, park one day. As
ran
hopped
I walked up to the park one day, So ear-ly in the morn-ing.
ran
hopped

Look at your hat!

Look at your hat!
Just look at your hat!
It's back to front
And squashed quite flat.
Look at your hat!

Look at your shirt!
Just look at your shirt!
It's inside-out
And covered with dirt.
Look at your shirt!

Look at your dress!
Just look at your dress!
It's rumpled and crumpled
And needs a press.
Look at your dress!

Look at your shoes!
Just look at your shoes!
They're full of holes –
Not fit to use.
Look at your shoes!

Look at your face!
Just look at your face!
It hasn't been washed.
What a disgrace!
Look at your face!

GO HOME!!

Look at your hat!

This verse also works well in pairs. One child speaks the verse, pointing to his partner as he speaks. His partner should respond with facial gestures only. Then she does the same to him with the next verse. This time he responds with a different facial gesture.

Movement rhymes and songs 3

Objectives

To encourage more formal corporate activity and involve circle formations and some 'dance' steps.

Level of development

Seven- to eleven-year-olds.

Classroom organisation

These songs and games will provide a good introduction to the dances suggested in the Singing and dancing games chapter. Encourage the children to make up their own verses and movements.

Slip one and two

Slip one and two
(*Children join hands in a circle and take two sliding steps to the left*)
Jump three or four
(*Make two little jumps. Drop hands*)
Turn around swiftly
(*Turn round once*)
And sit upon the floor
(*Sit on the floor with legs crossed*)
Clap one and two
(*Clap twice*)
Nod three and four
(*Nod twice*)
Jump up again
(*Jump up*)
And be ready for more.
(*Join hands again ready for the next time*)

The farmer

Adapted from a traditional song from Haiti.

We'll all clap hands and turn around
Please show us what to do
We'll all help the farmer with this work.

Leader
I'm milking, I'm milking
I'm milking now you see.

Everyone
He's milking, he's milking
He's milking now you see.

Children stand in a circle. One child stands in the middle as the 'farmer'. Everyone claps hands and turns around on the beat as they sing. The farmer chooses what work she is going to do and sings about this doing the appropriate actions. Everyone joins in and imitates what she does. She then chooses another child to go into the centre. Work through two to three more activities for the 'farmer' to do. Choose another child to go in the centre and select a different kind of work to dramatise – a policeman, shopkeeper, teacher, painter, nurse, etc.

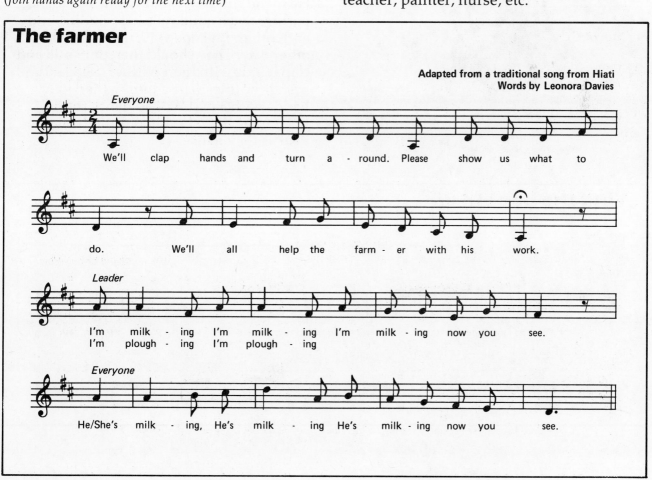

The farmer

Adapted from a traditional song from Hiati
Words by Leonora Davies

We'll clap hands and turn a - round. Please show us what to do. We'll all help the farm - er with his work.

Leader
I'm milk - ing I'm milk - ing I'm milk - ing now you see.
I'm plough - ing I'm plough - ing

Everyone
He/She's milk - ing, He's milk - ing He's milk - ing now you see.

Slip one and two

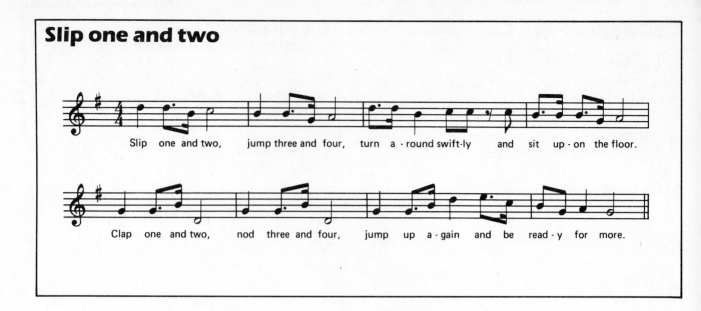

Slip one and two, jump three and four, turn a-round swift-ly and sit up-on the floor.

Clap one and two, nod three and four, jump up a-gain and be read-y for more.

Simple circle games will provide a good introduction to some of the more complex singing and dancing games suggested in this book.

Wind the bobbin up

Wind and wind the thread
And wind and wind the thread
And pull, pull, tap, tap, tap
One, two, three, come dance with me
One, two, three and off we go.

Have the children stand in lines facing a partner. Each child rolls her hands round each other, first one way, then back the other way. They should then pull, pull and clap hands with their partner. Repeat the first three lines. The children then join hands with a partner and dance round. Encourage them to skip or to step on the beat as they dance.

Wind the bobbin up

Danish singing game

Tune A

Wind and wind the thread and wind and wind the thread and pull, pull, tap, tap, tap.

Tune B

One, two, three, come dance with me, One, two, three and off we go.

Chants and songs 1

Objectives

These enjoyable 'nonsense' chants are often heard in the playground. They provide opportunities for developing rhythmic and co-ordination skills. 'Little Peter rabbit' and 'John Brown's baby' provide opportunities for internalising beat and melody.

Level of development

Six- to nine-year-olds.

Classroom organisation

These are all fun activities and the primary purpose in introducing them, at least initially, should be for sheer enjoyment. The lyrics of songs often provide useful starting points for teaching specific language concepts. For example in 'A sailor went to sea sea sea' you might like to point out the two different ways of spelling the words 'sea' and 'see'.

Little Peter rabbit

(to the tune of 'Glory Glory Alleluia')

Little Peter rabbit
(*Hands up behind head like ears*)

Had a fly upon his nose
(*Wiggle fingers towards nose. Repeat first two lines twice*)

And he flipped and he flapped it
(*Flip one way then the other*)

And it flew right away
(*Wiggle fingers away from nose*)

Poor old little Peter rabbit
(*Repeat twice*)

And he flipped it and he flapped it
And it flew right away . . .

Sing the whole song through the first time with the appropriate actions. The next time leave out the word 'nose' but do the action. Then leave out the words fly and nose. Next time leave out fly, nose and rabbit.

21

Little Peter rabbit.

A sailor went to sea sea sea

A sailor went to sea sea sea
To see what he could see see see
But all that he could see see see
Was the bottom of the deep blue sea sea sea.

A sailor went to chop chop chop
To see what he could chop chop chop
But all that he could chop chop chop
Was the bottom of the deep blue chop chop chop.

A sailor went to knee knee knee
To see what he could knee knee knee
But all that he could knee knee knee
Was the bottom of the deep blue knee knee knee.

A sailor went to sea, chop, knee
To see what he could sea, chop, knee
But all that he could sea, chop, knee
Was the bottom of the deep blue sea, chop, knee.

For the first verse salute three times on sea
sea sea. For the second verse do a chopping
movement three times. For the third verse
tap your knee three times and for the
fourth verse salute, chop, tap, three times.

John Brown's baby
(to the tune of 'Glory Glory Alleluia')

John Brown's baby got a cold upon his chest,
(*Repeat twice*)
So they rubbed it with camphorated oil
Camphor-amphor-amphor-ated,
(*Repeat twice*)
So they rubbed it with camphorated oil.

Sing it the first time with no actions.
The second time omit 'baby' and rock arms
instead. The third time omit 'baby' and
'cold' and add cough. The fourth time omit
'baby, cold, chest' and add tap chest. The
fifth time omit 'baby, cold, chest' and
'rubbed' and add rub chest. The sixth time
omit 'baby, cold, chest, rubbed' and
'camphorated oil' and add hold nose.

One finger, one thumb

One finger, one thumb, keep moving,
One finger, one thumb, keep moving,
One finger, one thumb, keep moving,
We'll all be merry and bright.

One finger, one thumb, one arm, keep moving . . .

One finger, one thumb, one arm, one leg, keep
  moving . . .

One finger, one thumb, one arm, one leg, one nod of
  the head, keep moving . . .

One finger, one thumb, one arm, one leg, one nod of
  the head, stand up, sit down, keep moving . . .

One finger, one thumb, one arm, one leg, one nod of
  the head, stand up, turn round, sit down, keep
  moving . . .

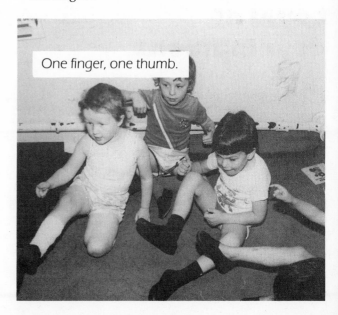

One finger, one thumb.

Chants and songs 2

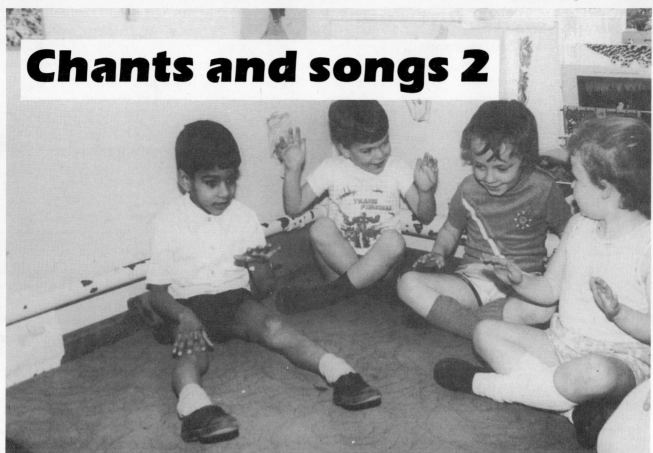

Objectives

Two contrasting chanting rhymes. 'Who stole the cookie' will demand rhythmic and co-ordination skills from the children. 'Vuka 'Ntombi Yam' offers opportunity for making up a sequence of verses to describe an activity or a job that people do.

Level of development

Seven- to eleven-year-olds.

Classroom organisation

These chanting rhymes can be introduced in the classroom. 'Who stole the cookie' is a fun game to play. It could be used at the beginning of term to help the children (and you!) learn names if you use children's names instead of numbers. 'Vuka 'ntombi yam' can be adapted to fit any sequential activity. Encourage the children to make up their own verses.

Who stole the cookie

A traditional West Indian chanting game. (I learned this version from children at a North London Primary School.)

Who stole the cookie from the cookie jar?
(*Everyone*)
Number 4 stole the cookie from the cookie jar
(*Leader*)
Who me?
(*Number 4*)
Yes you
(*Everyone*)
Not I
(*Number 4*)
Then who?
(*Everyone*)
Number 6 stole the cookie from the cookie jar
(*Number 4*)
Who me?
(*Number 6*)
Yes you
(*Everyone*)
Not I
(*Number 6*)
Then who?
(*Everyone*)
Number 2 stole the cookie from the cookie jar etc.
(*Number 6*)

23

Have the children sit or stand in a circle and number off round the circle. Set up a hand clapping pattern to establish and then keep the pulse – for example by slapping knees then clapping. Begin by chanting the verse together as a group. Then the leader (number 1) chooses the first 'culprit'. The game continues as indicated with each person trying to off-load the 'blame' onto someone else until someone misses a beat or slips up. He then turns round and faces outside the circle but continues to keep the pulse beat. Everyone begins chanting the verse again from the beginning. The trap now is to remember which number is 'out'. This gets more difficult as the game progresses. Each time someone is out try beginning at a faster speed. Always set the pulse going before beginning the chant.

Vuka 'ntombi yam (Get up my girl)

A traditional Zulu game song.

Leader
Vuka 'ntombi yam

Everyone
Vuka vuka vuka vuka
Vuka Vuka 'ntombi yam

Leader
Hamba 'ntombi yam

Everyone
Hamba hamba hamba hamba hamba
Hamba hamba 'ntombi yam.

'Vuka (vooka) means get up; 'ntombi yam' (ntoh-mbee yahm) means my girl. Substitute these words in succession for 'vuka':

2 Hamba – go to the river
3 Hlamba – wash in the river
4 Amanzi – carry water home on your head
5 Phemba – make a fire
6 Pheka – cook and stir food in pot
7 Phaka – serve the food
8 Bonga – give thanks
9 Yidla – eat.

The children should stand in a circle. Choose one child to stand in the centre and 'act' out the instructions. Choose another child to sing the 'leader'. As she sings this bar she steps into the circle, then back again. Everyone sings the rest of the song.

Using the same idea the children can make up, sing about and act out other sequential activities appropriate to their everyday life.

Chants and songs 3

Objectives

Two nonsense chants full of rhyming fun to be sung for sheer enjoyment.

Level of development

Five- to seven-year-olds.

Classroom organisation

Children will find these chants easy to learn because of their repetitious language and rhythmic structure. 'Miss Polly had a dolly' can be sung as well as chanted. You or your children (or their parents) might know the tune.

Miss Polly had a dolly

Miss Polly had a dolly
(*Fold arms and rock them*)
Who was sick, sick, sick
So she phoned for the doctor
(*Dial and hold phone*)
To be quick, quick, quick
The doctor came
With his bag and his hat
(*Swing one arm and carry a bag*)
And he rapped at the door
(*Knock at door*)
With a rat-a-tat-tat
He looked at the dolly
And he shook his head
(*Look serious and shake head*)
Then he said 'Miss Polly
Put her straight to bed'
He wrote on a paper
(*Write on the palm of one hand*)
For a pill, pill, pill
'I'll be back in the morning
(*Wave goodbye*)
With my bill, bill, bill.'

25

Miss Mary Mac

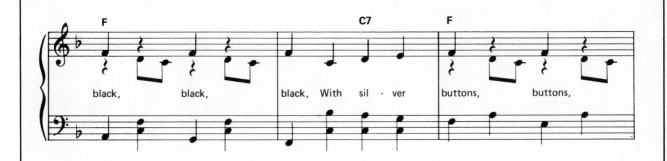

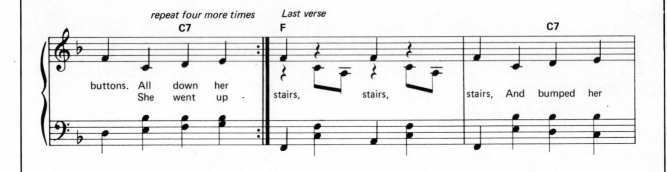

Miss Mary Mac

Miss Mary Mac, Mac, Mac,
All dressed in black, black, black,
With silver buttons, buttons, buttons,
All down her back, back, back.

She cannot read, read, read,
She cannot write, write, write,
But she can smoke, smoke, smoke,
Her father's pipe, pipe, pipe.

She asked her mother, mother, mother,
For fifty pence, pence, pence,
To see the elephant, elephant, elephant,
Climb up the fence, fence, fence.

He climbed so high, high, high,
He reached the sky, sky, sky,
And never came back, back, back,
Till the fourth of July, -ly, -ly.

She went upstairs, stairs, stairs,
And bumped her head, head, head,
And now she's DEAD.

Let the children make up their own clapping patterns.

Partners face each other and chant the rhyme. Let them try to work out some hand clapping actions together. They can either keep the pulse beat or they try to work out more complicated patterns (see also clapping games page 75). Can your class tell you from the lyrics from which country this chant originated? Have the lyrics been altered in any way?

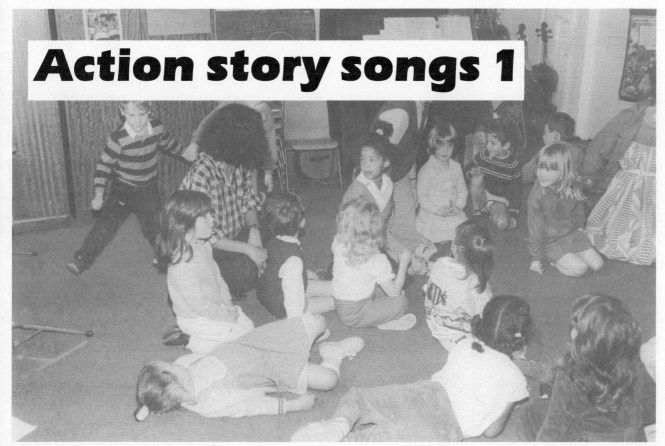

Action story songs 1

Objectives

These songs illustrate sequential ideas in order to tell a narrative or to describe processes in related activities. Learning to construct narrative ideas both orally and in written form, in a sequential order, is an important process in the development of children's linguistic skills.

27

Children enjoy dramatising songs about animals.

Level of development

Seven- to eleven-year-olds.

Classroom organisation

The repetitive nature of these tunes makes them easy to learn. The movements can therefore be introduced at the same time as the lyrics. Encourage the children to make up their own songs and movements based on these songs.

If I could have a windmill

If I could have a windmill
A windmill, a windmill
If I could have a windmill
I know what I would do.

I'd have it pump some water, some water, some water,
I'd have it pump some water all up from the river below.

And then I'd have a duckpond, a duckpond, a duckpond,
And then I'd have a duckpond, for ducks and geese to swim.

The ducks would make their wings flap, their wings flap, their wings flap,
The ducks would make their wings flap, and then they would say 'Quack, quack.'

The geese would stretch their long necks, their long necks, their long necks,
The geese would stretch their long necks, and then they would answer 's-s-s-s!'

The repetitive use of language makes this an easy song to learn. Let the children work out movements or actions to dramatise the significant ideas in each verse. Use the structure and patterning of these verses to encourage the children to make up a sequence of their own. They can use the same tune or they can make up their own tune using the rhythm of the original.

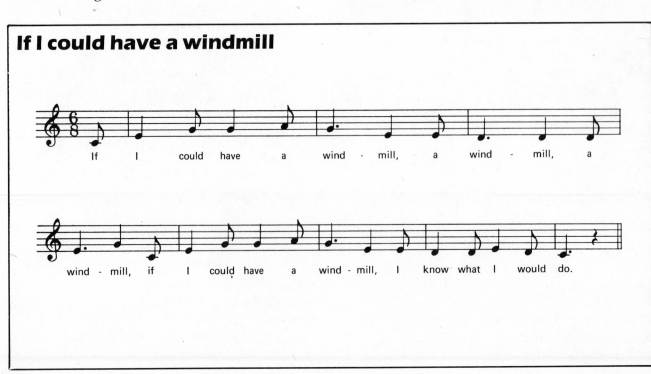

If I could have a windmill

If I could have a wind - mill, a wind - mill, a
wind - mill, if I could have a wind - mill, I know what I would do.

The water fairies

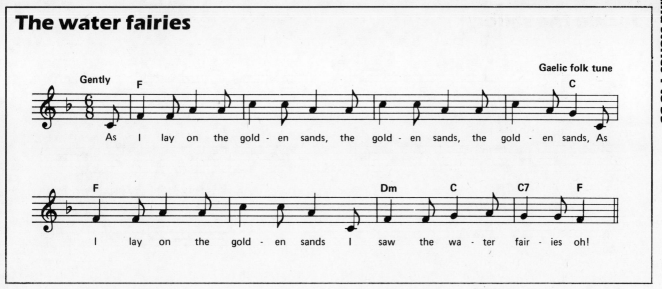

Gently

F

Gaelic folk tune

C

As I lay on the gold - en sands, the gold - en sands, the gold - en sands, As

F

Dm   C   C7   F

I lay on the gold - en sands I saw the wa - ter fair - ies oh!

The water fairies

As I lay on the golden sand
The golden sands, the golden sands
As I lay on the golden sand
I saw the water fairies oh!

The fleecy clouds sailed overhead
So snowy white and airy oh!

I watched the bonny seagulls fly,
A-wheeling o'er the water oh!

The sparkling waves came splashing in,
Each ridden by a fairy oh!

They danced across the shining sands,
In fairy rings so lightly oh!

They sang the sweetest fairy tune,
As hushed I lay a-listening oh!

And singing still, they flew away,
Like thistle-down a-floating oh!

This beautiful lilting folk tune comes as a
welcome contrast to some of the more
boisterous action and movement rhymes
and songs. After teaching the song, let the
children work in small groups to improvise
and create their own gentle water dance.
Use the idea of repetition in the words to
repeat a movement or dance step.
Encourage the children to listen to and to
move to the feel of the 6/8 rhythm.

Jackie the sailor

Oh Jackie is a sailor bold,
On a great big ship and a very fine ship,
Oh Jackie is a sailor bold,
And he spends his life at sea.

Chorus:
Oh Jackie is a sailor bold,
And he spends his life at sea.

He scrubs the deck to make it clean,
It's a great big ship and a very fine ship,
He scrubs the deck to make it clean,
And he spends his life at sea.

Chorus

He turns the wheel to keep the course,
It's a great big ship and a very fine ship,
He turns the wheel to keep the course,
And he spends his life at sea.

Chorus

He pumps out water when it leaks,
It's a great big ship and a very fine ship,
He pumps out water when it leaks,
And he spends his life at sea.

Chorus

He rows to the shore when the ship's in port,
It's a great big ship and a very fine ship
He rows to the shore when the ship's in port,
But he spends his life at sea.

Chorus

Use this sea shanty to make up a simple
horn-pipe dance. Make up different actions
to illustrate the different activities in each
verse. Do this in time to the strong pulse
which underlies the melody.

29

Jackie the sailor

Oh — Jack-ie is a — sail-or bold, On a great big ship and a ve-ry fine — ship, Oh — Jack-ie is a — sail-or bold, And he spends his life at sea. Oh — Jack-ie is a — **Chorus** sail-or bold, And he spends his life at sea.

Action story songs 2

Objectives

'There was a princess long ago' uses simple actions which help to develop a narrative. It can be developed in a variety of ways using movement, drama and other story-telling ideas. This work has important links to language development and in helping children to structure and to sequence their narrative ideas in a logical framework.

Level of development

Five- to six-year-olds.

'He took the princess by the hand . . .'

Classroom organisation

As this version is based on a well-known fairy story, you may wish to tell the story before introducing the song. Some teachers like to alter the words to the song (have the princess rescue the prince!) to make it less sexist. Ask the children to select parts of the story to make into a 'play'.

Verse 1 – Choose a 'princess' to go into the centre of the circle. Everyone else walks round as they sing.

Verse 2 – Everyone mimes the pricking of the finger.

Verse 3 – 'Princess' lies down and everyone puts their head down.

Verse 4 – Everyone in the circle gradually grows up as tall as they can.

Verse 5 – The 'prince' comes riding in and everyone tries to prevent him from getting into the circle.

Verse 6 – He gently touches one or two of the 'trees' and rides into the circle.

Verse 7 – As he touches the 'princess' she wakes up.

Verse 8 – Everyone dances round quite freely as they sing.

Follow-up

Use the idea of a narrative to make up other 'stories' in the same way. Combine other movement ideas with a 'narrative event'. Use the same tune, ie 'Some boys and girls played in the park, in the park, in the park . . . ;' 'They sat on the swings going up and down, up and down, up and down . . . ;' 'They zoomed down the slide going very fast, very fast, very fast . . .' etc.

These suggestions are starting points. Encourage the children to think of and to develop their own ideas.

There was a princess long ago

Verse 1 – There was a princess long ago
Verse 2 – She pricked her finger with a pin
Verse 3 – She fell asleep for a hundred years
Verse 4 – A great big forest grew around
Verse 5 – A handsome prince came riding
          by
Verse 6 – He chopped the trees down one by
          one
Verse 7 – He took the princess by the hand
Verse 8 – And then we all danced happily.

There was a princess long ago

There was a prin-cess long a-go long a-go long a-go. There was a prin-cess long a-go Long a-go.

Action story songs 3

Objectives

An opportunity to combine singing and story telling with actions.

Level of development

Five- to seven-year-olds.

Classroom organisation

Encourage the chldren, once they are familiar with the tune and the words, to develop their own ideas for dramatising this song. How will they show the different sizes of the bowls, the chairs and the beds? Encourage the idea of getting quieter and quieter in the last verse and then really loud at the end.

Goldilocks and the three bears

Chorus:
When Goldilocks went to the house of the bears,
Oh, what did her blue eyes see?

A bowl that was huge and a bowl that was small,
And a bowl that was tiny and that was all,
And she counted them – one, two, three.

A chair that was huge and a chair that was small etc.

A bed that was huge and a bed that was small etc.

A bear that was huge and a bear that was small
And a bear that was tiny and that was all,
And they growled at her Roar! Roar! Roar!

'A chair that was huge . . .'

33

The bear hunt

This is a longer and more involved narrative structure which combines with the additional dimension of sequencing sounds. It provides children with an important framework within which they can begin to acquire and develop confidence and control.

One morning a little boy
(*Stretch and yawn*)
Woke up, stretched, yawned
Got out of bed
Ooooooh Ooooooh
(*Wobble finger in mouth*)
He said, as he frightened his Mum,
'I'm going out for a walk.'
'I'm going on a bear hunt.'
He went out of the house.
Bang. He shut the door.
(*Clap*)
He walked down the road.
(*Tap hands on knees*)
'Who wants to come on a bear hunt?'
(*Speak this in rhythm*)
'I do'
After a while he came to a deep wide river.

'Who wants to come on a bear hunt?'
(*Speak this in rhythm*)
'Got to cross the river. Can't go through it.'
'Can't go into it, got to go over it.'
So he looked for a bridge.
He looked up the road.
(*Shade eyes and look one way*)
He looked down the road.
(*Shade eyes and look the other way*)
But there was no bridge.
'Who wants to come on a bear hunt?'
(*In rhythm*)
'Got to cross the river'
'Can't go through it. Can't go into it.'
'Got to go over it. No bridge'
'Got to go into it.'
So he dived into the water
(*Make diving movements with hands and head*)
And he swam splish splash
(*Make swimming movements*)
Splish splash to the other side
When he got out on the other side
He shook all the water off
Brrrrrrrr
(*Shake like a dog*)
On the other side of the river was a swamp.
'Who wants to come on a bear hunt?'

'Who wants to come on a bear hunt?'

(*In rhythm*)
'I do. How am I going to get through this swamp?'
'Can't go round it. Can't go over it'
'Got to go into it'
'Ugh' . . . his feet went
Squelch, squelch, squelch.
(*Pull up hands from knees*)
Then he came to a forest.
There was an enormous tree.
He looked round one side of it.
(*Peep round one side*)
He looked round the other side of it.
(*Peep round the other*)
Then he saw a cave.
'Who wants to come on a bear hunt?'
(*In rhythm*)
'I do'.
'Here's a cave. Can't see into it.'
'Can't see through it, can't see round it.'
'Better creep into it . . .'
(*Build next piece up very gradually*)
Very slowly he crept into it . . .
He listened . . . nothing there . . .
Suddenly in the darkness . . .
There was . . .
A . . . great . . . big . . .
Grrrrrrrr . . .
It was a BIG BROWN BEAR!
'Who wants to come on a bear hunt?'
(*Very quickly do everything in reverse order as fast as the children manage*)

'Not me . . .'
The little boy ran as fast as he could
he came to the big tree
He looked round one side
He looked round the other side of it
Then he came to the swamp.
'How am I going to get through this swamp?'
(*Speak in rhythm as fast as possible*)
'Can't go round it. Can't go over it.'
'Got to go through it'
'Ugh' His feet went
Squelch, squelch, squelch
Then he came to the deep wide river
'Where's the bridge?'
'No bridge'
'Got to cross the river'
'Can't go through it. Can't go over it.'
'Got to go into it'.
And he dived into the water.
He swam. Splish splash
As fast as he could . . .
He got out on the other side.
He shook all the water off.
Brrrrrrrr
He ran down the road as fast as he could.
He opened the front door.
He closed it
BANG
'Ooooh. Ooooh,' he said
'Who wants to come on a bear hunt?'
'NOT ME' . . .

Resources

Bright Ideas Language Development Frankie Leibe, Scholastic Publications (1984)

Okki-tokki-unga: actions songs for children compiled by Beatrice Harrop, A & C Black (1976)

Rhyme Time compiled by Barbara Ireson, Beaver Books (1977)

This Little Puffin compiled by Elizabeth Matterson, Puffin (1969)

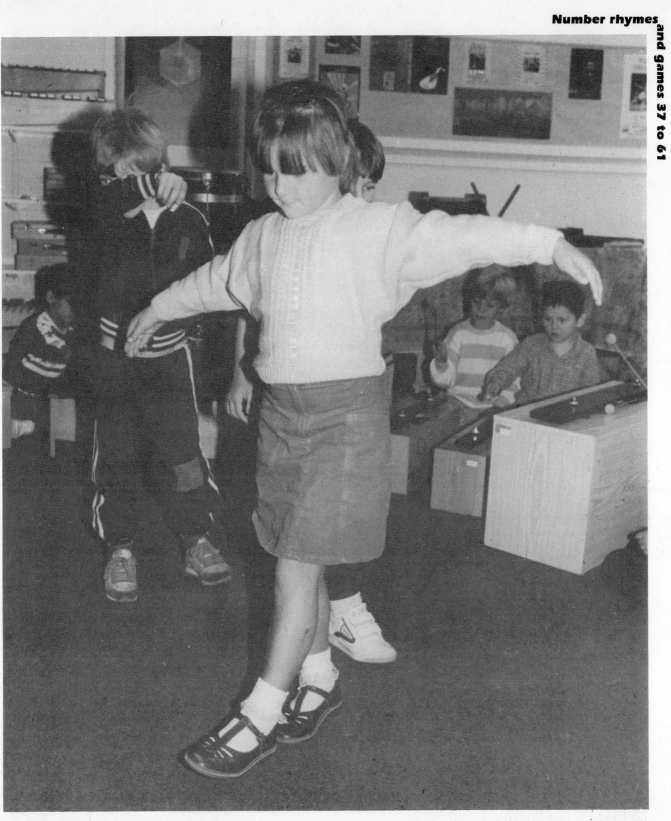

Number rhymes and games

Number rhymes and games

INTRODUCTION

Julia Matthews was head teacher of an Inner London Infant/Nursery school for many years. She co-directed a School Council Project of 'Early Mathematical Experiences' and at present has a Research Fellowship at the Froebel Educational Institute. In 1982 she obtained her doctorate with a study of the difficulties encountered by six- to seven-year-olds in written subtraction. She believes firmly in the importance of laying good mathematical foundations and that this can best be best achieved in a friendly atmosphere with the mathematics related to the children's other activities.

Numbers should be fun. They have many and versatile uses throughout life and it is essential that first encounters with them should be pleasurable. However, they can be frightening mumbo-jumbo to young children if not enough practical experiences have been provided before more formal use is demanded.

How can you help to make numbers 'fun' and, hopefully, turn out 'numerate' children? Certainly making friends with numbers is a prerequisite to numeracy. This can be done through games and activities that are related to the child's world. In addition, a fund of ear-catching rhymes and games is an invaluable asset for those odd moments that occur in the classroom. For many children in school these rhymes and games are part of their tradition, often a link between home and school. For minority groups they represent an insight into part of their adopted country's history.

The use of language and rhythm, not to mention the social value of sharing experiences, are all part of speaking in unison. These reasons alone are sufficient for teachers to perpetuate and perhaps add to their fund of rhymes and games. An added spin-off comes when, at times, some of these are followed up in order to reinforce an underlying mathematical concept. Follow-up activities may arise quite spontaneously but, on the whole, they are more valuable if planned beforehand and are used after the class has become reasonably familiar with the rhyme. As many children as possible should be involved, by repeating the activity with different sets of children.

To take an example, counting on and counting back become more meaningful if real children or objects are being counted. Without practical experiences counting is reduced to merely a matter of learning sounds in a certain order. A firm foundation for learning to count is given by matching and ordering 'things' to number names (one, two, three . . . and first, second, third . . .).

Another simple example is counting in two's which, of course, is a forerunner of the multiplication table. If a rhyme shows sets (or 'groups') gradually being built up, then it is perhaps a little simpler for children to comprehend that the answer to 'how many sets of 2?' is *not* 8, but 4 if the *total* is 8.

However, the reinforcement of mathematical concepts, desirable though this may be, is *not* the main aim of the contents of this chapter. The abstraction of mathematics comes from a wide variety of experiences: rhymes and games are just *one* source. They should be remembered by children with affection and help to provide them with the feeling that 'numbers are fun'.

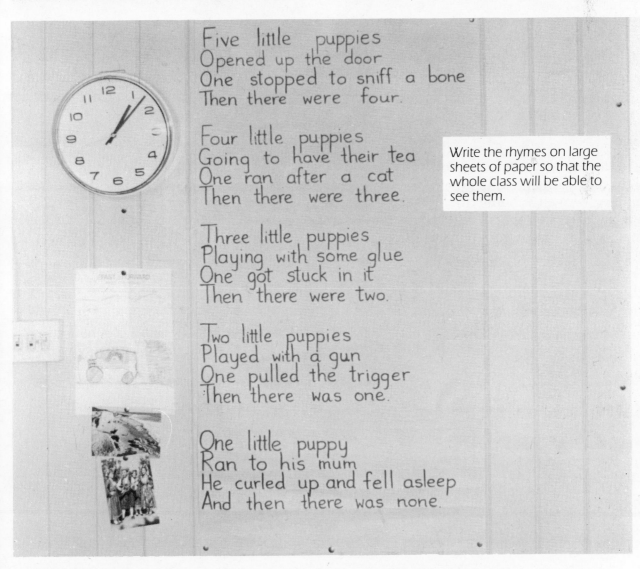

Five little puppies
Opened up the door
One stopped to sniff a bone
Then there were four.

Four little puppies
Going to have their tea
One ran after a cat
Then there were three.

Three little puppies
Playing with some glue
One got stuck in it
Then there were two.

Two little puppies
Played with a gun
One pulled the trigger
Then there was one.

One little puppy
Ran to his mum
He curled up and fell asleep
And then there was none.

Write the rhymes on large sheets of paper so that the whole class will be able to see them.

Counting

The following rhymes are intended to help children to learn and remember the order of counting, as well as being fun in themselves. Follow-up activities have been suggested for two of the rhymes: 'Number one' and 'Galloping horses'. Most of the other rhymes may be similarly developed to reinforce use of counting skills. The intended age range is between five and seven years but, naturally, the rhymes would appeal to older less able children with learning difficulties and to children with English as a second language.

Number one, touch your tongue

(see also page 42)

Objectives

Recognition of symbols one to ten and the ordering of numbers one to ten.

Level of development

On the whole this rhyme is most suited to children who have just started school. However, it must be accepted by teachers that, depending on the child's previous experiences, some older children may need help in recognising symbols also. The rhyme is a lively one, calling for matching actions so that there is no reason why it should not be used for at least the first two years of schooling.

Classroom organisation

Ten cards should be prepared beforehand, each about 160 cm × 120 cm, each showing a symbol one to ten. It is helpful to have a number line, either bought or home-made, with just the numbers one to ten on it.

The rhyme should be said once or twice

just for the pleasure of hearing the words and matching actions to them. Give ten children a numbered card to hold against their body with the number concealed. They should stand in the appropriate place on the number line so as to reinforce the children's ordering skills. As the rest of the group says the rhyme slowly, the 'number holder' turns the card round for all to see and the appropriate actions are carried out.

Follow-up

Once the rhyme is well known, you could pick a number card at random and ask the class to say the appropriate line and to mime the action, eg if '7' is picked the children say 'Number seven, point to heaven.'

A further follow-up in which all the class could take part, would be to make a large wall frieze, illustrating each number with the children's own pictures.

Galloping horses

(see also page 44)

Objectives

This rhyme will help children to learn the number bonds of ten. It is important for children to have certain facts at their fingertips and the learning of number bonds, certainly to ten, is one of the prerequisites of addition. Learning facts only by rote has not proved to be either satisfactory or lasting in the past. It is more profitable as well as being pleasurable to learn number bonds in a variety of ways.

Level of development

This lilting jingle can be enjoyed by most children between the ages of five and seven but the activities suggested are probably most useful for six- to seven-year-olds. Certainly it would be prudent to make sure that the children had acquired the concept of the conservation of number before reinforcing number bonds.

'They galloped up and they galloped down.'

Classroom organisation

The rhyme should be repeated once or twice with all the group/class 'galloping' on the spot. Then choose five children to be the white horses and another five to be brown. Ask the children to gallop in from a set place (eg the doorway) in single file and then turn off, five galloping up and then back along one side of the room and five along the other. They then gallop 'off' in single file, with the white ones leading the way.

Follow-up

The children could help to make ten 'horse' faces, coloured white one side and brown the other.

Repeat the rhyme as before but this time change the second line to 'Six were white and four were brown.' Have the children hold the faces up showing six white and four brown. Eventually all the combinations of ten could be 'galloped' through:

10 white and no brown
9 white and 1 brown
8 white and 2 brown
7 white and 3 brown
6 white and 4 brown
5 white and 5 brown
4 white and 6 brown
etc . . .

If you wish you could then ask the children to record in their own books the various combinations of ten.

Number one, touch your tongue

(for discussion see page 40)

Number one, touch your tongue.
Number two, touch your shoe.
Number three, touch your knee.
Number four, touch the floor.
Number five, learn to jive.
Number six, pick up sticks.
Number seven, point to heaven.
Number eight, shut the gate.
Number nine, touch your spine.
Number ten, do it again!

'Number three, touch your knee . . .'

'Two join hands . . .' (Ten merry men)

This old man

This old man, he played one
He played knick-knack on my thumb.
With a knick-knack paddy whack, give a dog a bone
This old man came rolling home.

This old man, he played two,
He played knick-knack on my shoe,
With a knick-knack etc . . .

This old man, he played three,
He played knick-knack on my knee,
With a knick-knack etc . . .

This old man, he played four,
He played knick-knack on my door,
With a knick-knack etc . . .

This old man, he played five,
He played knick-knack on my hive,
With a knick-knack etc . . .

This old man, he played six,
He played knick-knack on some sticks,
With a knick-knack etc . . .

This old man, he played seven,
He played knick-knack up in heaven,
With a knick-knack etc . . .

This old man, he played eight,
He played knick-knack on my plate,
With a knick-knack etc . . .

This old man, he played nine,
He played knick-knack on my spine,
With a knick-knack etc . . .

This old man, he played ten,
He played knick-knack once again,
With a knick-knack etc . . .

Ten merry men

Here are ten merry men,
(*Hold up your fingers*)
See how they dance and play:
(*Move your fingers*)
Two stand straight,
(*Forefingers*)
Two join hands,
(*Thumbs*)
The rest they run away.
(*Tuck away rest of fingers*)

One, two

One, two,
Buckle my shoe;

Three, four,
Shut the door;

Five, six,
Pick up sticks;

Seven, eight,
Lay them straight;

Nine, ten,
A big fat hen;

Eleven, twelve,
Dig and delve;

Thirteen, fourteen,
Maids a-courting;

Fifteen, sixteen,
Maids in the kitchen;

Seventeen, eighteen,
Maids a-waiting;

Nineteen, twenty,
My plate's empty!

43

Bell horses

Bell horses, bell horses
What time of day?
One o'clock, two o'clock,
Three and away.

Bell horses, bell horses,
What time of day?
Four o'clock, five o'clock
Time now to stay.

St Ives

As I was going to St Ives,
I met a man with seven wives.
Every wife had seven sacks,
Every sack had seven cats,
Every cat had seven kits.
Kits, cats, sacks and wives,
How many were going to St Ives?

(the answer is one!)

Galloping horses
(for discussion see page 41)

Ten galloping horses came to town,
Five were white and five were brown.
They galloped up and they galloped down,
And then they galloped right out of town.

Sausages

One day a boy went walking
And went into a store.
He bought a pound of sausages
(*Choose a few children, say six*)
And laid them on the floor.

The boy began to whistle
A merry little tune
And all the little sausages
Danced around the room.

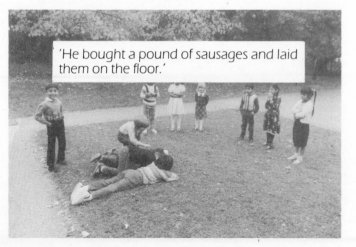

'He bought a pound of sausages and laid them on the floor.'

Fishes

One, two, three, four, five,
Once I caught a fish alive.
Six, seven, eight, nine, ten,
Then I let it go again.

Why did you let it go?
Because it bit my finger so,
Which finger did it bite?
This little finger on the right.

Ten tall soldiers

Ten tall soldiers
Standing in a row.
(*Hold up ten fingers*)
Five stood up
(*Lift one hand higher, spreading fingers wide*)
And the others lay low.
(*Make a fist with the other hand*)
Along came the sergeant
And what do you think?
Up popped the other five
Quick as a wink.
(*Open both hands and raise them high*)

'Up popped the other five quick as a wink!'

Five little owls

Five little owls in an old elm tree,
Fluffy and puffy as owls could be,
Blinking and winking with big round eyes,
As the big round moon that hangs in the sky.
As I passed beneath I could hear one say,
There'll be mouse for supper, there will today.
Then all of them hooted, tu-whit! tu-who!
Yes, mouse for supper, hoo, hoo, hoo, hoo!

Barbara Ireson

Seven little children

Seven little children
Running down the lane
Paddling in the puddles
Splashing in the rain.
Talking to each other
About the showery day
Seven little children
Going out to play.

(Repeat with walking, hopping, skipping etc.)

One, two, three, four

One, two, three, four,
Mary's at the cottage door;
Five, six, seven, eight,
Eating cherries off a plate.

Two, four, six, eight

Two, four, six, eight,
Meet me at the garden gate.
If I'm late, don't wait,
Two, four, six, eight.

How to write numbers

Learning to write numbers does not come easily or naturally to all children. It is a skill that should be taught at a fairly early age, say five or six years, before bad habits can be formed. The jingle, 'Number one, number one', may help and at the same time be light-hearted enough to encourage a comfortable feeling of familiarity, even friendliness, with the numbers.

Objective

To learn to write numbers correctly.

Level of development

Five- to six-year-olds, although the jingles may appeal to even younger children who are particularly interested in numbers.

Classroom organisation

Introduce only one number at a time. After repeating the jingle several times as a class activity, get the children to practise large bold movements in the air, using their hand or finger to 'draw' the number. The next step is to transfer this on to paper, using a thick pencil and a large sheet of plain paper. Lined paper should be avoided at this stage as the lines are usually a distraction to the child.

Although there is no reason why the whole class couldn't be involved in the activity of writing the number, it is much easier to supervise a smaller group to make sure that the children are 'drawing' correctly.

Follow-up

A different number should be tackled each day for a few minutes only, and when all the numbers have been gone through and the jingles learned, each child could choose his 'favourite' number to write and illustrate with a picture. This could then be made into a 'Class book of numbers'.

Number one, number one

Number one, number one
Now our rhyme has just begun,
From top to bottom – no trouble at all,
Draw me straight and thin and tall.

Number two, number two,
I'm the next for you to do.
I start at the top just like a swan's head,
And I sit on a straight line for my bed.

Number three, number three,
Start at the top to copy me.
A short straight line and down we go,
Then round at the bottom like a saucer you know.

Number four, number four,
Three straight lines then no more.
Start at the top, come down and along,
Cross with a straight line, you can't go wrong.

Number five, number five,
Start at the top then take a dive,
Bring your pencil nicely round,
And finish at the bottom all safe and sound.

Number six, number six,
This little number's full of tricks,
Start at the top, without a straight line.
Keep nice and curvy. Hey that looks fine.

Number seven, number seven,
Two straight lines like number eleven.
But start at the top with a line that's flat,
Then slope to the bottom and that is that.

Number eight, number eight,
Start at the top but no lines straight,
Down and out and round and back,
Like the shape of a pussy cat.

Number nine, number nine,
Looks like a big ball on a line.
Start at the top go round then straight,
Down to the bottom. It's simpler than eight.

When you've learned the way to do,
These nine numbers through and through,
Then any number that we know,
You can write it . . . just like so.

J. Matthews

Calling in, one-by-one

The following collection of rhymes are fun in themselves but they also serve a very useful purpose, mathematically, by matching in a one-to-one correspondence a number with either an action, a child or even a child pretending to be an animal.

One little elephant

(see also page 49)

These two 'elephants' are waving their trunks while pretending to balance on a piece of string.

Objectives

Matching in a one-to-one correspondence, each child to a number name. This activity, linked with many similar experiences, will help to prevent children just chanting numbers (or number words) and will help to link the numbers with the correct number of objects – in this case, children pretending to be elephants. The ordinal names (first, second, third . . .) are also used in the follow-up activity.

Level of development

Five- to six-year-olds.

Classroom organisation

It helps to have a piece of rope (or string) about six metres long for the children to balance on.

After the first verse has been repeated two or three times, choose one child to be the first elephant. She should start to 'balance' very slowly along the string, which has been placed on the floor to form a ring. Ask the class to repeat the verse; when they reach the final line, the 'elephant' should invite another child to join her. The second elephant follows the first one slowly 'balancing' and the rhyme is repeated until seven children are involved. Then the final verse is said. On the word 'snap' the class should clap their hands loudly and the elephants fall down.

The activity can be repeated with a different set of children or, if the class is in the hall or other large space, you could have several elephant rings proceeding at the same time.

Follow-up

You will need to make seven cards, each bearing a large ordinal number (eg 'first', 'second', 'third', etc). Repeat the activity as above but this time give the first 'elephant' the seven cards. When he chooses the second 'elephant', he retains his own card marked 'first' and hands over the other cards to the second 'elephant'. She, in turn, retains her 'second' card and hands the rest over to number three etc. At the end of the rhyme when the elephants have all fallen down, you could ask them all to stand up in a line with their cards in order and have the class join in, reading the cards aloud.

Peter works with one hammer

(see also page 49)

Objectives

Matching in a one-to-one correspondence to five and learning the numbers one to five.

Level of development

Five- to six-year-olds.

Classroom organisation

This activity is great fun either for the whole class or for a group to take part in together. Just when excitement appears to be getting too high, the final verse 'Peter's very tired now' puts them all 'to sleep'.

Obviously, the 'rules' must be spelled out first otherwise things might get out of hand. When teaching the rhyme it is easiest to select just one child to be Peter, while the rest say the rhyme. When they are all familiar with the actions the whole class can join in.

Have the children sit in a ring on the floor. Make sure there is plenty of space around each child. The first 'hammer' they tap with is the right hand (it is not really important which hand they start with!). The second is the left hand, so both hands are 'hammering', the third and fourth are the

Working with 'five hammers' takes a considerable amount of co-ordination.

two feet, one after the other, and the fifth hammer is the head nodding (NOT banging on the floor!). Make sure that the class knows the verse 'Peter's very tired now' signals absolute quiet with everyone 'sleeping' on the floor, and only you saying the words. On the last line the children should sit up quickly.

Follow-up

You will need six large cards, one with a picture of Peter sleeping and the others numbered one to five. Have the class say the rhyme through first, with the accompanying actions. Then hold up a number, eg '3'. The class must then repeat just the verse referring to the 'three hammers', so that the children are hammering with both hands and one foot. Repeat this several times, using different numbers. The 'sleep' card comes in very handy to hold up if things get a little too boisterous.

One little elephant
(for discussion see page 47)

One little elephant balancing,
Step by step on a piece of string,
Thought it was such tremendous fun,
That he asked another little elephant to come.

Two little elephants balancing,
Step by step . . .
(*Go on until, say, seven little elephants, then the verse changes*:)

Seven little elephants balancing,
Step by step on a piece of string,
Thought it was such tremendous fun,
But *snap* went the string and they all fell down.
(*Children tumble to the ground*)

The grocers

One grocer worked hard weighing rice,
Two grocers worked hard packing spice,
Three grocers worked hard sorting teas.
Four grocers worked hard wrapping cheese.
Five grocers worked hard stacking jam,
Six grocers worked hard slicing ham.
Seven grocers worked hard cutting meats.
Eight grocers worked hard opening sweets.
Nine grocers worked hard selling bread,
Ten grocers tired out went home to bed.

Barbara Ireson

Peter works with one hammer
(for discussion see page 48)

Peter works with one hammer, one hammer, one
   hammer,
Peter works with one hammer all day long.

Peter works with two hammers, two hammers, two
   hammers,
(*etc . . . up to five hammers, then:*)

Peter's very tired now, tired now, tired now . . .
Peter's WIDE AWAKE now!

Five little spacemen

Five little spaceman sitting on the stars,
The first one said 'Let's all fly up to Mars.'
The second one said 'There are rockets in the air.'
The third one said 'But we don't care.'
The fourth one said 'Let's go up in the sky.'
Then swish went the ship and out went the light,
And the five little spacemen flew right out of sight.
(*Hold up five fingers and point to each in turn. On the last line both hands make a rocket swish.*)

'But snap went the string and they all fell down' (One little elephant)

Nine little children
One little, two little, three little children,
Four little, five little, six little children,
Seven little, eight little, nine little children
All going out with their dad, dad.
Then one little, two little, three little children,
Four little, five little, six little children,
Seven little, eight little, nine little children –
Got sent back for being bad – that's sad!

J. Matthews

49

Ten little monkeys

One little monkey climbing up a tree.
Two little monkeys paddling in the sea.
Three little monkeys playing on a swing.
Four little monkeys skipping in a ring.
Five little monkeys drinking cherryade.
Six little monkeys digging with a spade.
Seven little monkeys rolling on the mats.
Eight little monkeys waving cricket bats.
Nine little monkeys nodding little heads.
Ten little monkeys sleeping in their beds.

Old Macdonald

Old Macdonald had a farm,
E-I-E-I-O
And on this farm he had some chicks,
E-I-E-I-O.
With a chick-chick here and a chick-chick there,
Here a chick, there a chick, everywhere a chick-chick.
Old Macdonald had a farm,
E-I-E-I-O.

Old Macdonald had a farm,
E-I-E-I-O
And on that farm he had some ducks,
E-I-E-I-O.
With a quack quack here etc . . .

Old Macdonald had a farm,
E-I-E-I-O
And on that farm he had some pigs,
E-I-E-I-O.
With a oink-oink here etc . . .

Old Macdonald had a farm,
E-I-E-I-O
And on that farm he had some mice,
E-I-E-I-O.
With a squeak-squeak here etc . . .
(*As many animals can be introduced as desired!*)

Dicky birds

One little dicky bird
Hopped on my shoe,
Along came another
And that made two.

Chorus:
Fly to the tree tops
Fly to the ground
Fly two dicky birds
round and round.

Two little dicky birds
Singing in a tree,
Along came another
And that made three.

Chorus

Three little dicky birds
Came to my door,
Along came another one
And that made four.

Chorus

Four little dicky birds
Perched on a hive,
Along came another one
And that made five.

Chorus

Let the children take turns being the farmer.

50

Counting down rhymes

Counting down rhymes encourage mental flexibility and most children enjoy the challenge of remembering the numbers 'backwards'.

There were ten in the bed

(see also page 55)

Objective

To make more meaningful the downward ordering of numbers by using the children themselves as the 'objects'.

Level of development

Six- to eight-year-olds.

Classroom organisation

After the class has become familiar with the words of the rhyme (it may also be sung), get ten children to lie side by side 'in bed'. With older children they could 'order' themselves by height before lying down so that the tallest is at one end and the shortest at the other. The rhyme is then repeated by the rest of the class and the children each roll away in turn. At the final verse, the 'little one' sits up and shouts 'I've done it – I've done it!' Repeat the game with a different set of children.

Follow-up

Prepare ten large cards each with a numeral, 0 to 10. String them together so that they can be flicked over. Appoint one child to be the 'conductor'. He is responsible for 'flicking over' the cards. The rest of the class must keep an eye on the conductor to make sure that the rhyme for the number revealed is said in unison. If the number showing is '8', for example, then two must roll out of the bed. They should roll back again at the end of the rhyme and wait to hear which number is called out next. If it is '6', then

51

These children found it easy to decide who was shortest and who was tallest but they weren't sure about those in the middle.

four should roll out of the bed to leave six in, etc. If '0' is shown they should all roll out. The chorus for '0' is 'There were none in the bed and no-one said roll over, roll over.'

'There were ten in the bed' lends itself very nicely towards art work. The children could draw a frieze showing first ten children side by side with the caption 'There were ten in the bed.' The next picture would show nine in the bed with one child rolling away, etc. The end picture would show the little one sitting up with the caption 'I've done it . . . .'

Five little mice
(see also page 54)

Objective
To reinforce the concept of 'one less'.

Level of development
Five- to six-year-olds (would suit nursery children also).

The five little mice creep timidly towards the cat.

Classroom organisation

This rhyme can be done either with a group or with the class. Choose five children to be the little mice and one child to be the cat. After all the children know the rhyme, they can act it out with the mice crawling from a corner and the cat 'catching' them one at a time and taking the captive back to his corner. Encourage the children to whisper the rhymes very softly during the acting (to prevent over-excitement when the cat pounces!) and even more softly and sadly for the last verse.

Repeat the activity with a different set of children, perhaps on another occasion.

Follow-up

Write the rhyme in large letters on a chart so that all the class can see it (start with just one verse). Point to the words as you say the rhyme to help the children follow along. You could prepare individual versions of the rhyme for each child which they could then illustrate. If you use a new page for each verse each child could have their own 'Five little mice' book. The numbers (both words and symbols) from five to zero could also be included.

Five lovely toys

(see also page 54)

Objective

To give children some experience in handling money, involving giving change.

Level of development

Six- to eight-year-olds.

Classroom organisation

Have a simple 'shop' counter with a few toys displayed. Put price tickets on each toy; use small amounts (eg all under 20p) to start with. Real money is essential. You will need plenty of pennies for change. Other currency can be introduced with older children. It is easier if you are the shopkeeper to start with. However, once the children are familiar with the game they could take turns. Have the group or class say the rhyme, and at the third line: 'Along came . . . with money to pay' the shopkeeper should name a child in the group and hand him some money to spend (eg a 20p piece). The child chooses a toy and you give him the necessary change. This can be counted out with great ceremony.

Choose another child to be purchaser and repeat the rhyme. Two or three children chosen to purchase at one session should be enough! You will need to make sure that the toys are labelled at different prices,

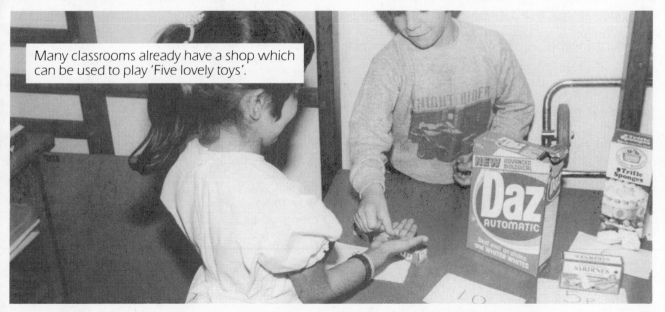

Many classrooms already have a shop which can be used to play 'Five lovely toys'.

depending on previous experiences of the children.

Follow-up

Older children could write simple 'bills' showing the toys bought, the amount tendered and the change given. Younger children could be asked to draw pictures.

'Phone for the doctor . . .' (Five little monkeys)

Ten green bottles

There were ten green bottles hanging on the wall,
Ten green bottles hanging on the wall,
And if one green bottle should accidentally fall,
There'd be nine green bottles hanging on the wall.

Nine green bottles hanging on the wall,
Nine green bottles hanging on the wall,
And if one green bottle should accidentally fall,
There'd be eight green bottles hanging on the wall.
(*etc . . . to last verse:*)

One green bottle hanging on the wall,
One green bottle hanging on the wall,
And if one green bottle should accidentally fall,
There'd be *no* green bottles hanging on the wall.

Five little monkeys

Five little monkeys bouncing on the bed
(*Bounce hand vigorously on knees*)
One fell off and bumped his head
(*Hold head and make a face*)
Phone for the doctor
(*Dial and hold phone*)
The doctor said
'Naughty little monkeys for bouncing on the bed.'
(*Hold up index finger in admonishing fashion*)

Four little monkeys bouncing on the bed etc . . .

Five little mice
(for discussion see page 52)

Five little mice came out to play,
Gathering crumbs up on their way.
Out came a pussy cat
Sleek and black,
Four little mice came scampering back.

Four little mice came out to play etc . . .

Five lovely toys
(for discussion see page 53)

Five lovely toys in a big toy shop,
Sitting on a shelf right on the top.
Along came . . . with money to pay.
(*call out child's name*)
Bought a . . . and hurried away.
(*car, plane, doll, ball etc*).

Four lovely toys in a big toy shop etc . . .

Balloons

Six balloons went off on a spree
High as a house, high as a tree,
To touch the sky they all did strive
One went pop! and that left five.

Five balloons went off on a spree,
High as a house, high as a tree.
Into the clouds they tried to soar.
One went pop! and that left four.

Four balloons went off on a spree,
High as a house, high as a tree.
Colours a-glowing so pretty to see.
One went pop! and that left three.

Three balloons went off on a spree,
High as a house, high as a tree.
Drifting along in a sky so blue,
One went pop! and that left two.

Two balloons went off on a spree,
High as a house, high as a tree.
They lifted their heads and looked at the sun.
One went pop! and that left one.

One balloon went off on a spree,
High as a house, high as a tree.
Felt very lonely and tired of the fun.
It went pop! and that left none.

Ten in the bed
(for discussion see page 51)

There were ten in the bed
And the little one said
'Roll over, roll over.'
So they all rolled over
And one fell out . . .

There were nine in the bed
(*etc . . . until last verse*:)

There was one in the bed
And the little one said,
'I've done it! I've done it!'

Ten miles from home

We're ten miles from home,
We're ten miles from home.
We walk a-while, we rest a-while,
We're nine miles from home.

We're nine miles from home,
We're nine miles from home.
We walk a-while, we rest a-while,
We're eight miles from home.
(*etc . . . to last verse*:)

And now we're home,
And now we're home.
We walked a-while, we rested a-while
And now we're home.

Five currant buns

Five currant buns in a baker's shop,
Round and fat with sugar on the top.
Along came . . . (*name of child*) with a penny one day,
Bought a currant bun and took it away.

Four currant buns in a baker's shop,
Round and fat with sugar on the top.
Along came . . . (*name a different child*) with a penny
   one day,
Bought a currant bun and took it away.
(*etc . . . to last verse*:)

No currant buns in a baker's shop,
Round and fat with sugar on the top.
Along came . . . (*name another child or yourself!*) with a
   penny one day,
No currant buns, so she/he went right away.

There were five in the bed and the little one said 'Roll over.' (Ten in the bed)

Ten fat sausages

Ten fat sausages sizzling in the pan,
Ten fat sausages sizzling in the pan.
One went pop and the other went bang,
There were eight fat sausages sizzling in the pan.

Eight fat sausages sizzling in the pan,
Eight fat sausages sizzling in the pan.
One went pop and the other went bang,
There were six fat sausages sizzling in the pan.
(*etc . . . to 'no fat sausages . . .'*)

Dinosaurs are a perennial favourite in the primary classroom.

Dinosaur

Ten awkward dinosaurs marching in a line;
One tripped and broke his neck: then there were
  nine.

Nine clumsy dinosaurs trying hard to skate;
One crashed right through the ice: then there were
  eight.

Eight gawky dinosaurs hitch-hiking through Devon;
One got lost on Dartmoor: then there were seven.

Seven bungling dinosaurs, keen on magic tricks;
One was really sawn in half: then there were six.

Six feckless dinosaurs learning how to dive;
One put no water in the tank: then there were five.

Five warlike dinosaurs joined the recce corps;
One couldn't read a map: then there were four.

Four reckless dinosaurs sailing on the sea;
A hungry shark swallowed one: then there were
  three.

Three demented dinosaurs in search of Doctor Who;
One argued with a Dalek: then there were two.

Two enterprising dinosaurs explored the Amazon;
One trod on a crocodile: then there was one.

One lonely dinosaur, when all his friends had gone,
Simply pined away and died: then there were none.

Charles Connell

Rhymes and teasers for older children

The following rhymes and teasers are mainly for older children. They are intended to help children feel at home with numbers and enable them to regard numbers as useful tools, over which they themselves have some control. They cover a wide spectrum, from the traditional rhyme giving the number of days in each month, to the rhyming teasers. The latter are intended to encourage logical thought. These can be given to individuals or pairs of children who you feel are able to rise to the challenge. They must, of course, be able to cope with the mathematical terms involved; for example it would be pointless to present a teaser about prime numbers to children who had not yet experienced these.

As a follow-up to the teasers, the children could try making up ones of their own to try on a friend. This may even necessitate making up a different rhyme for their new data.

Thirty days hath September

(see also page 59)

Objectives

A catchy jingle such as this one helps children to remember things they might otherwise forget. The activity suggested below will help to encourage graphical work.

Level of development

Seven- to ten-year-olds.

Classroom organisation

The rhyme may be familiar to some children

beforehand but it bears repetition and a current calendar would be a useful optional extra. The rhyme should be written out for classroom display. Get the children to discuss ways of showing the number of days in the months and lead them towards a bar graph, to begin with. Suitable graph paper must be chosen and the scale decided upon. A graph could then be built up with help from the written rhyme.

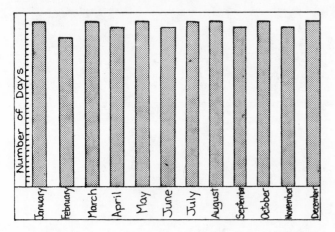

Further discussion of the graph will be necessary to pull out relevant information, eg

4 months have 30 days.
1 month has 28 days (or 29 if a leap year)
7 months have 31 days.
How many more months have 31 days than 30 days?
How many days altogether?
$(4 \times 30) + (1 \times 28) + (7 \times 31)$

Follow-up

One way to follow up this work would be to find at least one other way of recording the same information, eg

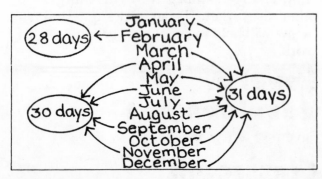

Work on the months could be extended to a more general project on the seasons (see page 94).

Odds and Evens

(see also page 59)

Objectives

This rhyme will help to give children confidence in identifying whether a number is odd or even. In itself, it may not seem very important to have to memorise this. However, to have grasped this knowledge can lead children to understand other facts. For example, if they add three odd numbers together accurately, the answer cannot be an even number, so the knowledge acts as a check. All prime numbers (except two) are, of necessity, odd numbers since all even numbers are divisible by two. To 'know' for sure is just another small step to getting children to feel comfortable with numbers and will certainly help them to recognise patterns and relationships in the world of mathematics.

Level of development

Seven- to ten-year-olds.

Classroom organisation

The rhyme should be repeated for just a few moments each day for as many days as it takes for the children to memorise it. A standard number line should be available, preferably permanently displayed around the room. Small groups or pairs of children can take turns testing each other by pointing to any number on the line for the rest of the group, or partner, to call out 'odd' or 'even'.

Follow-up

You will need to have a number board (eg up to 100). Alternatively the board to a game such as Snakes and ladders could be used. Two players put their counters half-way along the board (on number 50). A dice is thrown in turn. An even number means a move forward and an odd number means a move back. The winner is the first player to reach either the 'start' or the 'finish'.

The game can be made more difficult by playing with two dice. The players must then add the numbers of the dice and move forwards if the sum is an even number or backwards if the sum is an odd number. As before the winner is the first to reach either a hundred or one.

1 and 1 are 2

1 and 1 are 2
That's for me and you.

2 and 2 are 4
That's a couple more.

3 and 3 are 6
Barley sugar sticks.

4 and 4 are 8
Tumblers at the gate.

5 and 5 are 10
Bluff seafaring men.

6 and 6 are 12
Garden lads who delve.

7 and 7 are 14
Young men bent on sporting.

8 and 8 are 16
Pills and doctor's mixing.

9 and 9 are 18
Passengers kept waiting.

10 and 10 are 20
Roses-pleasant, plenty!

11 and 11 are 22
Sums for brother George to do.

12 and 12 are 24
Pretty pictures, and no more.

C. Rossetti

Thirty days hath September
(for discussion see page 57)

Thirty days hath September,
April, June and November.
All the rest have thirty-one
Excepting February alone,
Which hath twenty-eight days clear
And twenty-nine in each leap year.

Any number board will do for playing the follow-up to Odds and evens.

Odds and evens
(for discussion see page 58)
Odd numbers: one, three, five, seven, nine
Find them on the number line.
What's left—zero, two, four, six, eight
Are evens you'll appreciate.
Learn these numbers off by heart
Then you'll be ready to play your part.
For any number, large as it may be,
The very last digit will give the key.
It's *odd* if it's nine, seven, five, three or one,
And *even* if it ends with any other one.

J. Matthews

Our famous counting law

Two and two add up to four,
And by our famous counting law
Three and two are just one more
And that makes . . .
(*Children call out the answer*)

Three and three add up to six
And by our famous counting law
Four and three are just one more
And that makes . . .

Four and four add up to eight
And by our famous counting law
Five and four are just one more
And that makes . . .

Five and five add up to ten
And by our famous counting law
Six and five are just one more
And that makes . . .

Five and five is ten
Now can't you guess
Five and four are just one less
And that makes . . .

Four and four is eight
etc . . .
to two and one . . .

J. Matthews

Favourite numbers

My favourite number happens to be eight,
I think eight is really great.
You just take four and then add four more
What does that make? EIGHT . . . great.
You try now, take five and three,
What does that make? EIGHT . . . great.
What about six and then add two,
What does that make? EIGHT . . . great.
Try one alone and then add seven.
What does that make? EIGHT . . . great.
Add all your fingers (don't count the thumbs)
What do they make? EIGHT . . . great!

(How about *your* favourite number?)

J. Matthews

Two cats

Two cats? –
Why! that's
Eight paws,
Two tails and
Forty claws.

Samuel Marshak

Farmer Jackson's farm

(How many lines can you say in one breath?
How long does it take to say the whole
rhyme?)

Farmer Jackson has on his farm:
one dog
two cats
three goats
four pigs
five hens
six cows
seven geese
eight ducks
nine sheep
ten lambs
– and hidden away where nobody sees a hundred
hundred honey-bees.

Clive Sanson

Two legs

Two legs sat upon three legs,
With one leg in his lap.
In comes four legs
And runs away with one leg.

Up jumps two legs,
Catches up three legs,
Throws it after four legs
And makes him bring back one leg.

(Two legs is a child; three legs a stool; one
leg a joint of meat and four legs a dog.)

Teasers

A three-digit number you must find
The smallest in front and the largest behind.
The middle digit you will see
Is four times the first and half digit three.
(*Answer 148*)

A two-digit number,
Not thirty – it's less.
The first you must square
For the second, I guess.
(*Answer either 24 or 11*)

A three-digit number am I,
My middle digit is the sum
Of my first and my last.
The whole number is divisible by eleven
And thirteen, for sure, but *not* by seven.
(*Answer 143*)

Think of a number between zero and nine
(Any of them will do just fine)
Double it, add one and then add four.
Double again and add two more.
Divide by four and take away three.
Your original number you should see.

Thirty-seven times thirty-three,
Use your calculator and you will see
Palindromic it will be.

Can you find any more,
With answers three-o-three, or four-double-o-four?

To the first digit add twice the second.
This gives the third, or so I've reckoned!
Try to do it in record time –
The completed number is a prime.
(*Answer 137*)

One, two, three, four, five, six, seven, nine
(Leave out the eight and you'll be fine)
Multiply by sixty-three
You'll be amused by what you see.

Find a two-digit number and call it 'me'
Multiply me by myself and you'll see
That the answer a three-digit number will be.
It's square and palindromic – that's the key.
(*Answer 121*)

Think of any number and see if you can square it,
Add twice the first number – if you can bear it.
Now add one, to give a perfect square.
What is it the square of? – the end is near.
From this new number, take away one
And you should be back where you'd begun.

Think of a number and then add five.
Multiply by ten – now look alive!
Take away fifteen, then by five divide.
Now add forty-one – write the answer at the side.
Divide by two and take away twenty-four
Is your first number there once more?

(Try another number)

Think of a number and multiply by three
Take away two, now double what you see.
Add four now, then divide by six.
That's juggling with numbers – making them do
  tricks.

J. Matthews

Let the children work in pairs with a calculator on the teasers.

Resources

Bright Ideas Maths Activities Julia Matthews, Scholastic Publications (1985)

Counting Rhymes Clive Sansom (Ed), A & C Black (1974)

Count Me in, A & C Black (1984)

Playground games

Playground games

INTRODUCTION

Frankie Leibe worked for ten years with an educational publishing company commissioning and editing books on early reading and language development skills. She left to become a freelance editor and writer. Her publications include *Bright Ideas Language Development* and *Bright Ideas Reading Activities*. She is now living in mid-Wales where she works as an educational arts adviser with an educational charity.

The school playground has a unique role to play in children's lives today. It is one of the few places where children of different ages can play together in groups which are culturally and socially mixed without the distractions of television, or the enticements of elaborate play equipment or adventure playgrounds. In the school playground children are left very much to their own devices; they are thrown back on their own resources and have to occupy themselves with a minimum of adult intervention or supervision.

These conditions make the school

playground the ideal place for the lore and language of school children – so ably described by the Opies in their book of the same name – to breed, grow and be passed on from one generation of children to another. Like the old playstreets, the playground is the place where children learn from each other the skills needed to participate successfully in the social world of childhood. These skills include a working knowledge of ritual, language and the 'informal game traditions' described by Arnold Arnold, ie those games which have been passed down from generation with no adult help and no written rules.

Most of the games included in this chapter are traditional ones. They have stood the test of time and many children will no doubt know some of them already (possibly with interesting regional variations); others will be delighted to meet them for the first time.

Language is an important element in many of the games played in the playground. The rhymes, chants or songs control the games through their rhythm and momentum. A variety of traditional and contemporary variations have been included here. No doubt the children will offer many more. Other examples of playground language can be found in the chapter on Nonsense rhymes (see pages 91 to 110).

Playground games are an important part of children's lives. Apart from the language skills they develop they also encourage physical skills – hand/eye co-ordination, agility, dexterity, running, jumping, catching, throwing – and they teach social skills which the children will need for adult life as well. In playing games the children learn to share, to take turns, to be part of a team, to win and lose graciously. They learn to make up, learn to abide by rules and how to deal with those who refuse to do so. They learn to abide by group decisions, and when to apply the powers of persuasion or precedent to change or modify rules and decisions. They learn when to capitulate and when to take a stand. In short, they learn, through playing games, how to get along with other people. (For a

Many playground games have been passed down from generations.

more detailed exploration of what children learn in the playground see Andy Sluckin's *Growing up in the Playground*.)

Most of these games can be played without the help of adults. However some of the other ones included here are more formal and will need direct supervision. The 'supervisor' may be an adult or an older child. In these games the children will be learning to work as part of a team not necessarily of their own choosing, to begin and end a game within a definite time limit and to abide by the decision of an impartial referee.

In most cases suggestions for sizes of groups have not been included. The age ranges are just as flexible. Many of the games are meant to be played by a range of ages and as many or as few children as care to join in. The rules are not rigid. The children may well choose to modify them to suit a particular time, place or age range.

Some examples have been given to show how the games can be used to complement, initiate, or follow-up classroom work. These are, of course, suggestions only and you will undoubtedly have many other ideas on how to use the playground games to underpin teaching points.

Skipping

Skipping is a perennial favourite in the playground which has recently received a boost thanks to the appearance of amazing speed skippers on television. There are lots of different variations for solo, pair or group skipping. The language of the rhymes generally deals with everyday items and occurrences and as such, they can all be used as starters for project work. Some suggestions for using 'Colours' and 'When is your birthday?' have been included here.

Colours
(see page 70)

Objectives
To teach children to recognise, name and differentiate between basic colours, and the various hues within colour groups.

66

Level of development

Five- to ten-year-olds.

Classroom organisation

With younger children, play 'Colours' as described on page 70 in the playground first, and make a note of the colour names the children call out. Later, in the classroom, gather the children together and ask them to tell you which colours they chose in the game and to point to something in the classroom which is that colour.

If they are confident about naming and matching colours, make a class graph to show the children's favourite colours and make 'colour corners' in order of preference, with each child either bringing in or finding something of the appropriate colour. You can go on to do work on the different hues within each colour. The children may well be able to offer light red, dark red etc. Try to encourage them to branch out into scarlet, vermilion, crimson, cherry etc. They could then make colour charts based on families, with all the different names.

When you play Colours again limit the children to choosing hues from just one or two colour families, eg the blues and greens.

Older children could start playing the game at the more sophisticated level, ie using just one colour family from the start.

Follow-up

Younger children could paint a giant rainbow for the classroom and do simple science work based on the spectrum. They could make graphs based on favourite colours, or colours of hair and eyes, and have a week of songs and stories based on colour: a splendid starter would be Charlotte Zolotow's *Mr Rabbit and the Lovely Present*; other favourites are Eve Rice's *New Blue Shoes*, Robert Graves' *The Big Green Book*.

Older children might enjoy finding out about colour blindness, and trying to make up their own colour blindness tests.

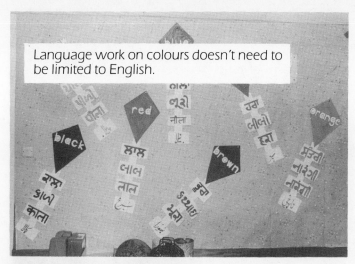

Language work on colours doesn't need to be limited to English.

When is your birthday?

(see also page 70)

Objectives

To teach children the months of the year as a basis for work on seasons and climate (see also classroom ideas for Thirty days hath September, page 57).

Level of development

Five- to ten-year-olds.

Classroom organisation

Before playing the playground game with young children, spend some time in the classroom making sure that the children know the month and day on which they were born. Make a simple 'birthday chart' showing the number of children born in each month and teach the order of the months by singing songs like Flanders and Swan's 'January brings the snow' or reading books like *January Jo*. Once the children are confident about the order of the months, you could divide the year into the seasons.

If the birthdays are reasonably evenly distributed, the 'spring' children could make a frieze, book or corner all about

This class of six-year-olds drew pictures of themselves to stick on their birthday graph.

spring, with pictures, collages, objects, poems, books etc, possibly linking colour with each season; all the other 'seasons' children could do the same. The Provensen's *A Year at Maple Tree Farm* is an excellent starter/reference book, and the newly reprinted *Flower Fairies* books of the different seasons are invaluable for plants of the various seasons.

Older children normally enjoy the hurly-burly of the skipping game as the year (and the skipping rope!) draws to an end. They could do classroom work making their own graphs to show the distribution of birthdays by month and day of the month. They also could break up into 'season' groups to do work on climate – looking at average temperatures, hours of sunshine, rainfall etc (see also page 94 for other weather-related activities).

Solo

Most of the rhymes, new and traditional, involve skipping to a rhyme which ends in the 'bumps' (turning the rope twice while jumping once) until the person is 'out', ie trips over the rope.

Salt, mustard, vinegar, pepper

This is perhaps the original skipping rhyme. The player chants the four-word rhyme

Salt, mustard, vinegar, pepper

and either just skips normally until out, does the bumps throughout or does the bumps on 'pepper' each time.

Down in the valley

Down in the valley where the green grass grows
Dear little . . . (*insert name*) she grows and grows
She grows and she grows and she grows so sweet
That she calls for her boyfriend down the street.
Simon, Simon, put your hat and coat on
How many kisses did she give him?
1,2,3 etc.
(*Skipper does the 'bumps' until out*)

Down in the valley where the green grass grows
There sits . . . washing her clothes
She sings, she sings, she sings so sweet
She sings to her playmate down the street.
Playmate, playmate, won't you come to tea
Come next Saturday at half-past three
There'll be ice-cream and cream cakes for you and me
Won't we have a lovely time at half-past three.

Bumps are a standard feature of most skipping games.

'Colours' is a simple but fun skipping game to play.

Bluebells, cockle shells

(For the first two lines the skipper swings the rope to and fro, jumping over it, and turns it fully over the head on 'over'.)

Bluebells, cockle shells
Eeevy, ivy over.
Daddy is a baker
He made a lovely cake
How many hours did it take?
1,2,3 etc.
(*Skipper does the 'bumps' until out*)

Nebuchadnezzar

This rhyme is a true test of fitness. The skipper does the bumps on the last word of each line, and does non-stop bumps for the 'Doh, ray' etc until out.

Nebuchadnezzar the King of the Jews
Bought his wife a pair of shoes
When the shoes began to wear
Nebuchadnezzar began to swear
When the swear began to stop
Nebuchadnezzar bought a shop
When the shop began to sell
Nebuchadnezzar bought a bell
When the bell began to ring
Nebuchadnezzar began to sing
Doh, ray, me etc.
(*Continue until player is out*)

Drip, drop

Drip, drop, down by the sea
Up popped a mermaid and she said to me
Please Sir tell me the time
Mind your own business it's half-past nine (*ten eleven, twelve etc*).
(*Whoever is skipping does the bumps until out*)

Apple crumble, apple tart

Apple crumble, apple tart
Tell me the name of your sweetheart
A,B,C,D etc.
(*Skipper continues until out and then has to name sweetheart whose name begins with the last letter*)

Pairs

Most games start with a solo skipper who then calls in a friend and they skip together.

I like coffee

I like coffee
I like tea
I like . . . (*whoever*) in with me
(*Friend runs in and they skip together*)

I don't like coffee
I don't like tea
I don't like . . . in with me
(*Friend runs out*)

Groups

There are lots of different skipping games for groups of children. A good one to start with is something simple which involves the children running in and out of the rope 'keeping the kettle boiling', ie without a gap between the players.

Under the moon and over the stars

Two children turn the rope. The rest of the group forms a line. The rope turns and as the turners shout 'under the moon' the line of children takes turns to run under the rope and line up on the other side. The turners then shout 'over the stars' and the line of children takes turns to jump over the rope. Anyone who misses a go or stops the rope becomes a turner.

Any player who touches the rope or misses a turn becomes a turner.

Colours
(for discussion see page 66)

Two children hold the rope and wriggle it to and fro so that it makes wide ripples. They each choose a colour, which they tell each other but not the rest of the children. The rest line up and take turns to jump over the rope, shouting the name of a colour as they do so. Anyone who calls out the colour which one of the turners has chosen then has to change places with the turner, who chooses a new colour, and so on. A simpler version of this game is 'Wriggling snakes'. The children jump over the rope in the same way but no colours are chosen. Anyone who misses a turn or touches the rope becomes a turner.

When is your birthday?
(for discussion see page 67)

Two children turn the rope, and call out, 'When is your birthday? Please jump in.' They then go through the months of the year in sequence and the rest of the group run in on their birthday month. When the turners reach December it then changes to 'When is your birthday? Please jump out' and the skippers run out on their birthday month.

Up and down the ladder

Two children turn the rope. The rest of the group gets into pairs. The first pair run in at opposite ends of the rope and while the rest of the group sings the rhyme, they skip up and down the length of the rope in opposite directions, passing each other in the middle, while the children sing:

Up and down the ladder, bom bom
The ladder, bom bom
The ladder, bom bom
Up and down the ladder, bom bom
Early in the morning.

If they stop the rope, they become turners. If they finish successfully they run out and the next pair run in. An alternative is for one child to run in and call out:

Two, four, six, eight
Calling . . . (whoever) at the gate.

The child whose name is called runs in to make the pair and the two children then sing 'Up and down the ladder' etc.

I am a Girl Guide

Two children turn, while the rest of the group takes turns to run in and skip, performing the actions.

I am a Girl Guide dressed in blue
Here are the actions I must do
Salute to the King
And bow to the Queen
And turn my back on the man in green.

I'm a little bumper car

Two children turn the rope, while one other skips.

I'm a little bumper car, number 48
I went round the corner
(*On this line the skipper runs out of the rope, round behind one of the turners and back in the other side*)

I stopped at the traffic lights
Pulled down my brake
A policeman came and caught me
And put me into jail
How many years did I stay?
1,2,3 etc.
(*Continue until the skipper is out*)

Jelly on the plate

Two children turn while a third skips and performs the actions.

Jelly on the plate
Jelly on the plate
Wibble wobble wibble wobble
Jelly on the plate.

Teddy bear

Two children turn while a third skips and performs the actions:
Teddy bear, teddy bear, touch the ground
Teddy bear, teddy bear, turn around
Teddy bear, teddy bear, climb up stairs
Teddy bear, teddy bear, say your prayers
Teddy bear, teddy bear, turn out the light
Teddy bear, teddy bear, say 'Good-night'
GOOD-NIGHT!
(*On the last 'good-night' the skipper runs out*)

All the girls in our town

All the girls in our town live a happy life
Except for little . . . (*whoever*) who wants to be a wife
And a wife she will be according to the name
Along with . . . (*boy's name*).

She kisses him she hugs him
She sits upon his knee
She says my darling will you marry me?
And the next Saturday morning the wedding shall be
Will she marry him? We shall see
Yes, no, yes etc.
(*Skipper does bumps until out*)

In 'Up and down the ladder' a pair of children skip up and down the length of the rope in opposite directions.

French skipping

This game is quite demanding in terms of physical coordination. Seven- to eight-year-olds may be able to manage the early stages but the later ones are best suited to older children.

Two children stand facing each other, about five feet apart, with a circle of elastic stretched round their ankles. A third player jumps in and out of the elastic in the sequence shown in the illustrations on page 73 to the following rhyme:

Jingle
Jangle
Centre
Spangle
Jingle
Jangle
and OUT!

A misjump, or the wrong action, means that player is out and one of the two 'post' children takes her place. If the player successfully completes a stage, she progresses to the next one until out.

Stage 1

The player jumps in and out of the elastic in the sequence illustrated:

1 with the elastic at ankle level
2 with the elastic at knee height ('kneesies')
3 with the elastic at thigh height ('underbums')
4 doing 'gallopsies', ie rapidly alternating feet throughout.

Jingle

Jangle

Centre

Spangle

Jingle

Jangle (and out)

Stage 2 'Thinsies'

1–4 as above but with the elastic stretched round one leg only.

Stage 3 'Widesies'

1,2,4 as above, but with the elastic round both legs, with legs straddled apart.

Stage 4 'Outsies'

1–4 as above, but the player has to jump outside the elastic after each move.

Stage 5 'Insies'

As in stage 4 above, but the player has to jump inside the elastic after each move.

Stage 6 'Diamonds'

1–4, but the player has to pick up one of the sides of the elastic with her foot at each stage, so making a diamond shape.

Stage 7 'Onsies'

1–4 as above, but the player has to land with one foot on the elastic at each move.

Stage 8

In the last stage, the player jumps in and out of the elastic chanting: 'England, Ireland, Scotland, Wales, centre, spangle, centre on and off.'

In Diamonds the elastic will make a diamond pattern with each jump.

Clapping games

These games, usually played by pairs of children, seem to have enjoyed a recent comeback. The traditional pattern is hands together, right palms, hands together, left palms, hands together, both palms, hands together etc, although variations have crept in. The rhymes again are a mixture of very traditional plus new variations. As the following example shows, they can be used in the classroom to help children develop a sense of rhythm.

Objectives

To teach children to recognise, and repeat, simple rhythm patterns.

Level of development

Five- to eight-year-olds.

Classroom organisation

All the playground clapping games can be used as either starters or follow-ups for teaching simple rhythm patterns. Sit in a circle with a group of children, clap a short simple rhythm pattern, eg three long claps. Ask the children to clap it back to you, then

ask individual children to clap it back.
Introduce another pattern, perhaps with
two short quick claps in between two long
ones. Again ask the children as a group and
then individually to clap it back. Once the
children have mastered quite complex
patterns, sing a song together, clapping in
time with the music. Start with well-known
nursery rhymes like Baa Baa Black Sheep, or
Humpty Dumpty. After singing the words
and clapping, just clap the rhythm of one of
them and see if the children can guess
which one it is. Once the children are
confident, ask individuals to clap out songs
and see if the rest of the class can guess what
they are from the clapping rhythm only.

Follow-up

The children could make a tape of clapped
songs to swap with another class to see how
many tunes they recognise.

If some children find the rhythm
difficult, pair them with a child who is
particularly adept and encourage them to
play some of the simpler clapping games
together (eg 'My mother said' or 'I'm
Popeye the sailorman').

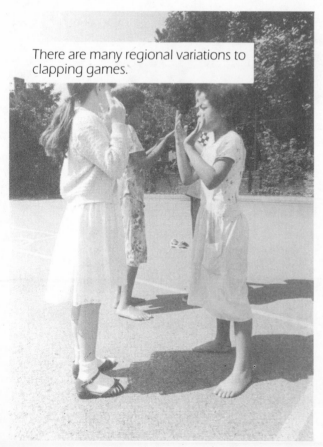

There are many regional variations to
clapping games.

My mother said

My mother said
I never should
Play with the gypsies
In the wood
If I did
She would say
Naughty little girl
To disobey
Your hair won't curl
Your shoes won't shine
You gypsy girl
You shan't be mine
The sky was blue
The grass was green
Along came Sally
With a tambourine
I saw a white horse
I upped on its back
Sally tell my mother
That I shan't be back.

See, see my baby

See, see my baby
I cannot play with you
Because I've got the flu
Chicken pox and measles too
Go down the drainpipe
Go down the cellar door
And that will leave you to
To shut the door
Don't say bore
Granny's gone to the shopping store.

Oh Mrs Ching Chong

My mother she told me to open the door
But I didn't want to
I opened the door and fell flat on the floor
Oh Mrs Ching Chong.
(*Hands together in prayer gesture, players wiggle
downwards*)

I went to a Chinese restaurant

I went to a Chinese restaurant
To buy a loaf of bread, bread, bread
(*Palm to palm only for 'bread, bread, bread'*)
I wrapped it up in a five pound note
And this is what I said, said, said
(*Palm to palm only for 'said, said, said'*)
My name is Chicolo Chicolo
Wee Willie Winkie
Tom Tom Tom Tom
Indian Chief.

For the first line of 'Oony dusty Anna' the players hold hands and swing them to and fro.

'1, 2, 3, 4, 5 I'm alive!'

Oony dusty Anna

(for the first line the players hold hands and swing their joined hands to and fro)

Oony dusty Anna
I said EastaWest
I met my boyfriend at the candy store
He bought me ice-cream
He bought me cake
He brought me home
With a belly ache
I said a Momma Momma
I feel sick
Call the doctor
Quick quick quick
Doctor doctor
Will I die?
Count to five
And you'll survive
1,2,3,4,5 (*alternate palms only*)
I'm alive! (*throw back hands, palms facing forwards*)

I'm Popeye the sailor man

I'm Popeye the sailor man
(*Two palm to palm claps at the end of each line*)
I live in a caravan
I opened the door
Fell flat on the floor
I'm Popeye the sailorman.

77

Ball games

There are many different ball games played in the playground. You and your class will no doubt be familiar with such favourites as 'Piggy in the middle' and 'Jump ball'. The ball games included here have been chosen because of their use of language. To show how even the simplest games can be used in the classroom ideas for extending 'Clock-face catch' have been included.

Clock-face catch
(see also page 80)

Objective
To teach young children to tell the time.

Level of Development
Six- to nine-year-olds.

Classroom organisation

As a preliminary to playing Clock-face catch, teach, or make sure the children know, the clock-face. The children could make their own clock-faces and draw in the numbers from one to twelve. Reinforce the hours by playing Clock-face catch, asking the child in the middle to throw to each of the hours in turn. Once the children are confident, call out the hours in random order.

In the classroom, teach the minute hand positions, beginning with the hour and half-past, then moving on to quarter past and quarter to. Reinforce each stage with a game of catch. Finally teach the in-between minutes.

Follow-up

Divide the class into two teams, with 12 children in each team. One team makes the clock-face, the other will be the 'hands'. Ask the 'hands' team to divide into pairs – one child to be the hour hand, the other the minute hand. Ask each pair to make a certain time, eg ten past two. The children then have to go and stand in the correct positions on the outside of the human clock-face. When one team has had several turns at telling the time, the two teams change positions.

Older children could use the same game to practise the 24-hour clock.

'One, two, three and upsy'

Two ball

The blank brick walls which are the despair of aesthetically minded teachers and parents can be a real asset for ball games. So many children now live in flats, terraced houses or semis that they have little chance to throw a ball up against a wall without causing havoc. If you are lucky enough to have a window-free wall, encourage the children to use it for 'two ball' games.

They can play on their own or in groups, taking turns to have a go. Apart from counting how many times they can throw the balls against the wall and catch them without dropping them there are different rhymes which can be used to help keep the rhythm going and bring in different variations.

Ollicka, bollicka

Ollicka, bollicka
Sillicka, sollicka
Ollicka, bollicka
Knob.

One, two, three

One, two, three and over
(*On 'over' the ball is thrown overarm*)
Four, five, six and over
Seven, eight, nine and over
Ten and over
Over ball.

One, two, three and upsy
(*On 'upsy' the ball is thrown up in the air*)
Four, five, six and upsy
Seven, eight, nine and upsy
Ten and upsy
Over ball.

One, two, three and dropsy etc.
(*On 'dropsy' the ball is thrown against the wall and allowed to bounce once before being caught*)

One, two, three and bouncy etc.
(*On 'bouncy' the ball is bounced from the ground onto the wall and then caught*)

One, two, three and backsy etc.
(*On 'backsy' the ball is thrown round the player's back*)

One, two, three and turnsy etc.
(*On 'turnsy' the player throws the ball and has to turn round once quickly before catching it*)

Catching and throwing games

These can be played with either a ball or a bean bag.

Clock-face catch

(for discussion see page 78)

Twelve children form a large circle, facing inwards to make the clock-face. Each child is given a number from one to twelve. One child stands in the middle. He has the ball or bean bag and throws it to each person in the circle in turn, starting with number one, who then throws it back to the centre. To begin with the children should call out the numbers as they go. Anyone in the circle who drops the ball changes places with the person in the middle.

When the children become more confident you could call out the hours and the child in the middle has to work out which person to throw the ball to.

'Queenie, Queenie who's got the ball?'

Queenie

One person is chosen to be Queenie and is given the ball (or bean bag). Queenie turns her back on the rest of the players and throws the ball over her shoulder. One of the players picks it up. The children then stand in a line with their hands behind their backs. When Queenie turns round they chant:

Queenie, Queenie, who's got the ball?
Is she big or is she small?
(*The children raise and lower one hand to act out big and small*)
See have I got it
(*The children show one empty hand, the other still behind their backs*)
See have I got it
(*They show the other empty hand. The person who has got the ball simply swaps hands quickly*)
Queenie, Queenie, who's got the ball?

Queenie then runs past the line of children shouting:
'Queenie's coming'
while they turn round quickly so she can't see their hands and turn quickly round again as she runs back shouting:
'Queenie's coming'

Queenie then has to decide who has the ball. She stands in front and eliminates the players by calling:

'Jenny, you're a dirty dustbin' (*meaning Jenny has not got it*)

until either she guesses the right player (who then becomes Queenie) or she eliminates everyone except the one who has got the ball. In that case Queenie remains the same and the game restarts.

A slight variation is to play the same game but call it 'Kingio'. The rhyme becomes:

'Kingio, Kingio, who's got the ballio? Is she smallio?'

And when Kingio runs past the children he shouts 'Kingio's coming through the gate' and 'Kingio's going out the gate' when he runs back.

Circle and group games

Most of these games are traditional. Generations of children have enjoyed them and still do so, especially younger children who are just learning to play in a group and take turns. Games which label the parts of the body such as 'Here we go Looby Loo' and 'Hokey Cokey' are an excellent teaching tool for use with young children as the example given in this section shows.

Here we go Looby Loo
(see also page 83)

Objectives
To teach the names of parts of the body and the difference between left and right.

Level of development
Five- to seven-year-olds.

Classroom organisation
Both Looby Loo and the Hokey Cokey are useful, letting-off-steam ways of teaching/reinforcing the names of different parts of the body and the difference between left and right.

A skeleton or string puppet can be used to teach the names of the different parts of the body, backed up with songs like 'Dem bones', 'Heads and shoulders, knees and toes' or 'One finger, one thumb keep moving' (see page 22).

The children can make and label themselves by lying on the ground and asking a friend to trace round them, and then drawing and labelling their head, arms, legs etc.

Once they are confident about parts of the body, move onto left and right. If it's winter the children could put 'L's and 'R's on the appropriate boot or glove. In the summer take the children outside to play Looby Loo or do the Hokey Cokey. Children who are still having difficulty might need extra practice through games like 'Simon says', or 'Follow my leader' or playing with the puppet or skeleton and making them do the various actions.

Follow-up

The ultimate test of co-ordination and knowing left from right is marching! Those children who are able may well enjoy marching along to brass band music, with an instructor asking them to halt and then start with the left leg, or right leg and alternate arm.

Once they know left from right, the children can be taken in small groups for road safety lessons, with the emphasis on looking right, left, right again (because British cars drive on the left).

The farmer's in his den

A group of at least ten children stand in a circle holding hands. One child is chosen to be the 'farmer' and he or she stands in the middle while the children circle round clockwise singing:

The farmer's in his den
The farmer's in his den
Ey-ay-adio the farmer's in his den.

The farmer wants a wife
The farmer wants a wife
Ey-ay-adio the farmer wants a wife.

(*The Farmer now chooses a wife from the circle of children. She joins him in the middle and they hold hands and circle round anticlockwise while the song continues.*)

The wife wants a child etc.

(*The wife chooses a child who then becomes part of the inner circle*)

The child wants a nurse etc.
(*The child chooses his nurse*)

The nurse wants a dog etc.
(*The nurse chooses her dog*)

The dog wants a bone etc.
(*The dog chooses his bone*)

We all pat the bone
We all pat the bone
Ey-ay-adio we all pat the bone.

(*All the children pat the poor bone, who then becomes the new farmer.*)

The compensation for being chosen to be the bone is that you get to become the new farmer.

Here we go Looby Loo

(for discussion see page 81)
The children join hands to make a large circle, and circle clockwise singing:

Here we go Looby Loo
Here we go Looby Light
Here we go Looby Loo
All on a Saturday night.

(The circle then stops and the children do the appropriate actions to the various verses)

You put your right arm in
You put your right arm out
You shake a little a little
And turn yourself about.

You put your left arm in etc.
You put your right leg in.
You put your left leg in etc.
You put your whole self in etc.

'Put your left foot in . . .'

Hokey Cokey

The same theme as Looby Loo but much noisier and more boisterous! Again the children make a circle, but without joining hands. They then sing and do the appropriate actions to the various verses.

You put your left arm in
Your left arm out
In out in out
You shake it all about
You do the Hokey Cokey
(Palms together and wiggle hips)
And you turn around
That's what it's all about.
Oh hokey cokey cokey
Oh hokey cokey cokey
Oh hokey cokey cokey
(While singing these three lines, the children join hands and run into the centre and back, twice)
Knees bend, arms bend, raa raa raa.

Children love the last three lines of the Hokey Cokey.

In and out the windows

The children form a circle and weave in and out as they walk round singing the verse. If they find it difficult to weave in and out, ask alternate children to stand still while the others walk round weaving in and out.

In and out the windows
In and out the windows
In and out the windows
As we have done before.

Stand and face your partner
Stand and face your partner
Stand and face your partner
As you have done before.
(The children stop and face whoever is opposite them)

Dance around together etc.
(The partners join hands and dance round together)

Shake hands before you leave her etc.
(The children shake hands in time to the music and then the game starts again with the first verse)

Very young children can play an easier version. The children stand in a circle, with joined hands held high to make the windows. One child is chosen to walk in and out of the windows while the verse is sung. When the second verse stops (ie 'Stand and face your partner') he stands and faces the nearest child and they then dance around together while the third verse ('Dance around together') is sung. For the final verse ('Shake hands before you leave him') they stand and shake hands. Choose another child to do the walking and repeat.

Poor Jenny sits a weeping

The children make a circle with joined hands. One person is chosen to be Jenny. She sits in the middle of the circle and pretends to cry while the others circle round clockwise singing:

Poor Jenny sits a weeping, a weeping, a weeping
Poor Jenny sits a weeping on a bright summer's day.

Oh tell us why you're weeping, you're weeping,
  you're weeping
Oh tell us why you're weeping on a bright summer's
  day.

(Jenny now sings)
I'm weeping for my sweetheart, my sweetheart, my
  sweetheart
I'm weeping for my sweetheart who's far far away.

The chorus answer:

Stand up and choose a new one, a new one, a new
  one
Stand up and choose a new one, on a bright
  summer's day.

(Jenny does so and the 'sweetheart' joins her in the centre where they dance round together as the rest of the children continue to circle and sing)

Now dance around together etc.

The 'sweetheart' then becomes the new Jenny.

In and out the dusty bluebells

The children form a large circle and stand facing the centre, without joining hands. One child is chosen to start the game. She or he walks round the circle, weaving in and out between the children who sing:

In and out the dusty bluebells
In and out the dusty bluebells
In and out the dusty bluebells
Won't you be my partner?

On 'partner', the child stands behind the nearest child in the circle and pats her or him on the shoulders singing:

Pat, pat, pitter patter
On your shoulder
Pat, pat, pitter patter
On your shoulder
Pat, pat pitter patter
On your shoulder
You shall be my partner.

The first child leaves his hands on the second child's shoulders and together they weave in and out of the circle while the first verse is sung and the game is repeated until all the children have become one long chain.

Wallflowers can be played by a small group or by the whole class.

Young children enjoy repeating such favourites as 'Ring a ring o' roses'

Ring a ring o'roses

This is perhaps one of the best known traditional ring games yet it is still popular with very young children. The children form a circle, with linked hands, and circle clockwise singing:

Ring a ring o'roses
A pocketful of posies
Atishoo, atishoo
We all fall down.
(*On 'down' the children bob down, either squatting or sitting, and remain there, while singing the second verse*)
Picking up the daisies
(*The children pretend to pick the flowers*)
Picking up the daisies
Atishoo, atishoo
We all jump Up!
(*On 'up' the children jump up to a standing position*)

Wallflowers

A group of children make a circle, with joined hands, and circle clockwise singing:
Wallflowers, wallflowers, growing up so high
We're all pretty maidens, we none of us want to die
Except for . . . (*whoever*), she's the only one
So turn her round and turn her round so she can't
  face the sun.
Whoever's name is called out turns round so she faces out of the circle, but continues to walk round still holding hands with the rest of the group. The verse is repeated until all the players are facing outwards.

I sent a letter to my love

The children sit or stand in a large circle. One person is chosen to be 'It'. She walks round the outside of the circle singing:

I sent a letter to my love
And on the way I dropped it
One of you has picked it up
And put it in your pocket.

It wasn't you, it wasn't you, it wasn't you . . .
(*The player continues going round and then either taps one of the other children on the shoulder or drops a hanky behind them and shouts*)
It was you!

At this the person chosen jumps up (if sitting) and runs round the outside of the circle after the first player. The first one back to the empty place stands or sits in it. The game then continues with the other child walking round the outside of the circle.

Sing a song of sixpence

This circle game based on the traditional nursery rhyme will appeal most to five- to six-year-olds.
  The children form a large circle with linked hands. Five children are chosen to be the King, Queen, blackbird, maid and Jenny Wren. Jenny Wren stays outside the circle,

85

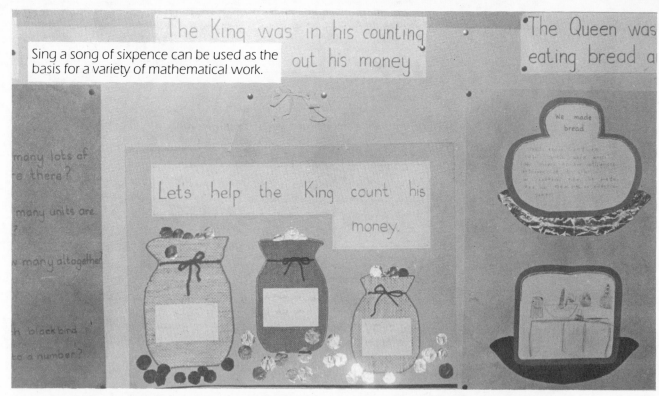

The King was in his counting out his money

The Queen was eating bread a

Sing a song of sixpence can be used as the basis for a variety of mathematical work.

We made bread

Lets help the King count his money.

many lots of
e there?

many units are
?

w many altogether

h blackbird
to a number?

while the rest of the characters stay inside.

Both circles of children hold hands and walk round (clockwise for the large outer circle, anti-clockwise for small inner circle) singing:

Sing a song of sixpence
A pocketful of rye
(*On 'rye' the outer circle crouch down*)
Four and twenty blackbirds baked in a pie
When the pie was opened
(*During this line the outer circle of 'blackbirds' gradually rise up, stop holding hands and start to flap their 'wings' while singing:*)
The birds began to sing
Now wasn't that a dainty dish to set before the king?

(*During the next verse the characters perform their actions:*)
The King was in his counting house
Counting out his money
The Queen was in the parlour
Eating bread and honey
The maid was in the garden
Hanging out the clothes
When down came a blackbird
And pecked off her nose.
(*The blackbird pecks off the nose by sticking her thumb between the first and second finger*)
She made such a commotion
That little Jenny Wren
Flew down into the garden
And stuck it on again.
(*Jenny Wren flies into the inner circle and puts the nose back on*)

Oranges and lemons

Two children form an arch with arms raised, holding hands. The rest of the children form a line and go through the arch while singing the traditional rhyme:

Oranges and lemons
Say the bells of St. Clements
I owe you five farthings,
Say the bells of St. Martins.
'When will you pay me?'
Say the bells of Old Bailey.
'When I grow rich'
Say the bells of Shoreditch.
'When will that be?'
Say the bells of Stepney.
'I do not know'
Says the great bell of Bow.
Here comes the candle to light you to bed
Here comes the chopper to chop off your head.
Chip, chop, chip, chop, CHOP!

On the final 'chop' the two children forming the arch bring their arms down to catch the child passing through. That child then has to choose whether to be an orange or a lemon, and lines up behind the appropriate player. When all the children have been allocated to the orange or lemon line, the two teams have a tug of war to decide which will be the winner.

Here we go gathering nuts in May

Divide the children into two equal groups. The groups face each other in two straight lines, holding hands. They then skip forwards and backwards singing:

Here we go gathering nuts in May, nuts in May, nuts in May.
Here we go gathering nuts in May, early in the morning.
(*One line then sings*:)
Who shall we choose to be Queen of the May, Queen of the May, Queen of the May.
Who shall we choose to be Queen of the May, early in the morning?
(*They then choose someone and sing*:)
We'll choose . . . (*whoever*) as Queen of the May, etc.
(*The other group then replies*:)
Who shall we choose to steal her away? etc.
(*They then choose someone and sing*)
We'll choose . . . (*whoever*) to steal her away etc.

The two teams then form human tug of war teams, with the Queen of the May and whoever was chosen to steal her away at the head of the teams.

When playing with young children, one time through the arch (made here by two children) is sufficient.

Oranges and lemons is a popular party game which can be played on the playground.

The big ship sails

The more players the better for this game. The children stand in a line holding hands. The first person in the line places his or her right arm up against the wall to form an arch. The last person in the line then leads the children round to file under the arch while singing:

The big ship sails on the alley, alley-o
The alley, alley-o, the alley, alley-o
The big ship sails on the alley, alley-o
On the last day of September.

As the line files through, the first player does a half turn to form a new arch with the next player. The children continue to file through, making half turns and new arches as they do so. When there are no more arches, the players unwind themselves by doing a half turn under their arms, starting with the last person in the line and working up towards the first singing:

The Captain said it would never never do
Never, never do, never, never do
The Captain said it would never never do
On the last day of September.

The big ship sank to the bottom of the sea
The bottom of the sea, the bottom of the sea
The big ship sank to the bottom of the sea
On the last day of September.

When everyone is unwound the children form a large circle, holding hands and facing inwards, point their right feet and lift them up and down to the music as they sing:

We all dip our feet in the deep blue sea
The deep blue sea, the deep blue sea
We all dip our feet in the deep blue sea
On the last day of September.

For younger children a simpler version can be used with children just following the leader through the arch and then holding hands to form a circle in the normal way for the last verse.

Resources

The World Book of Children's Games Arnold Arnold, Macmillan (1975)

The Lore and Language of School Children Iona and Peter Opie, Oxford University Press (1959)

Inky Pinky Ponky: collected playground rhymes Michael Rosen and Susanna Steele, Granada (1982)

Growing up in the Playground: the social development of children Andy Sluckin, Routledge & Kegan Paul (1981)

Blue Bell Hill Games R A Smith, Puffin (1983)

Nonsense rhymes and jingles

Nonsense rhymes and jingles

INTRODUCTION

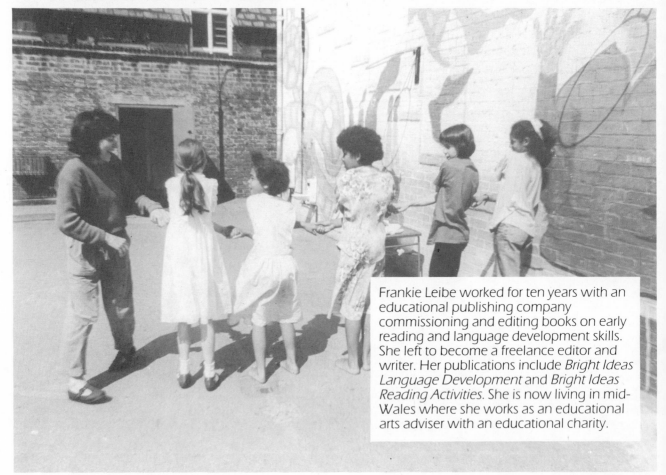

Frankie Leibe worked for ten years with an educational publishing company commissioning and editing books on early reading and language development skills. She left to become a freelance editor and writer. Her publications include *Bright Ideas Language Development* and *Bright Ideas Reading Activities*. She is now living in mid-Wales where she works as an educational arts adviser with an educational charity.

Helping children to develop their spoken language skills is one of the most important tasks facing primary school teachers: learning and teaching are both dependent upon communication, and speech is the way most of us choose to communicate with each other.

How can we best help children to develop these skills? Rhyme, rhythm and repetition, plus music, all make language easier to acquire, remember and reproduce. It is precisely these qualities which television advertisers exploit so successfully in their jingles, as shown by the fund of commercial ditties many children master long before they have acquired much else in the way of spoken language skills. There is

nothing wrong with young children learning these jingles – the more they listen, memorise and repeat the better. It just seems a waste not to extend their budding skills beyond rhymes designed to sell breakfast cereals! We need to offer them alternative, equally attractive material to play with. As this chapter shows there is a wealth of material – both traditional and contemporary – on which to draw.

Enjoyment is the other important factor. Children need to practise their spoken language skills: if they enjoy using language they will practise through playing with it, as babies and toddlers do. Most children have a keen sense of the ridiculous. They love jokes and dreadful puns so humour or nonsense is an excellent form of motivation.

The first sections of this chapter therefore include a large proportion of nonsense among the rhymes and jingles. The rhymes are divided into sections by general topics, eg People, Animals etc. Much of the material is traditional and will probably appeal to children between the ages of four and seven.

The section on tongue twisters will work better with slightly older children. They will enjoy trying to get their tongues round the sounds, which might defeat younger children. They will also appreciate the humour of the idiosyncrasies of the English language whereby words which have completely different meanings and spellings can sound identical.

The final three sections consist of rhymes, jingles and nonsense which children themselves have made up and used for generations. Here we see language which children have appropriated for themselves and which they may or not wish to share with adults (indeed some adults wouldn't want to have it shared with them!). There is a seemingly endless supply of material when you take into account all the regional variations: you and your children will be familiar with some of the ones here, and will no doubt know many more.

As these rhymes have been developed by children for children, they are useful starting points for getting children to explore and experiment with language. For this reason they have been included in this book even though some are rather rude. Sometimes it is necessary to come down to the children's level to help them appreciate the great variety of language available.

Dips are an integral part of many playground games (see page 63). They are used to decide who will be 'It', 'on it' or leader of the game. Many have been in use for generations; parents and grandparents will be able to supply many more. Rhymes and jingles are also used in the playground as part of rituals like making up after a quarrel, promising to tell the truth, to be said on certain days of the year etc.

The last section contains just a few of the songs and stories which can be heard in the playground. Some, like 'The worm song' and 'Oh Jemima' may well be old friends. Others, like 'My daddy is a dentist' are newcomers: it is the children who decide whether they will stand the test of time.

As mentioned earlier, music is an important element both in helping children to memorise rhymes and in adding to their enjoyment of them. Much of the material included in this chapter is meant to be sung or chanted. Where possible the names of the well-known tunes have been included. As with the language of the songs and rhymes, there may be regional variations in the tunes used.

Many nonsense rhymes are meant to be sung or chanted.

Classroom use

Most of the nonsense rhymes and jingles included in this chapter originated in the playground (or playstreet) and that is where they will continue to breed and grow for future generations to enjoy. They can, however, also be used in the classroom. A few examples have been given to show how the material might be developed. The suggestions are deliberately open ended, as is the material itself. The emphasis is on using the nonsense rhymes, jingles etc as starters to spark the children's own sense of fun in playing with language. In many cases the enjoyment is an end in itself; in others it is a useful spur to more detailed project work. You will no doubt have many other ideas of how best to use the material with the children.

Nonsense rhymes

The weather
(see also page 97)

Objective
To develop a 'language' starter for a project on weather.

Level of development
Eight- to eleven-year-olds.

Classroom organisation
Use the nonsense rhymes as a 'starter' for other rhymes/sayings about the weather. See what the children come up with either off the top of their heads or from looking through books of folklore, quotations, or by asking parents etc. They will gradually build up a collection, no doubt including such old favourites as:

Red sky at night, shepherd's delight
Red sky in the morning, shepherd's warning.

Mackerel sky, mackerel sky
Sometimes wet, sometimes dry.

If on St Swithin Day it rain
For forty days shall do the same.

Sun before seven
Rain before eleven.

Shed not a clout till May is out.

March winds and April showers
Make way for sweet May flowers.

These sayings could be made into a class book, complete with illustrations. Encourage the children to include explanations for the origins of the sayings and, if possible, some personal examples of the truth or otherwise of each saying.

Follow-up
The 'Weather folklore book' could be used as part of a long-term project on weather, especially if it were combined with the

seasonal information gathered as suggested on page 67. It might be possible to exchange the information with another school in a different part of the country, or even a different country, to compare not just the technical information, but also the different weather lore.

Special days
(see also page 97)

Objective
To help the children make a calendar of 'special days', using simple research and recording techniques.

Level of development
Five- to eleven-year-olds.

Classroom organisation
Younger children will probably enjoy all the rhymes given here. Older children may well prefer the first! Whatever the age of the children, these rhymes could be used as the basis of a 'Special days' calendar for the class. Apart from birthdays, younger children could find out about, and either write or tape, information about New Year's Day, Pancake Tuesday, Ash Wednesday, April Fool's Day, Halloween, the summer and winter solstices etc. Religious festivals and holidays, such as Easter, Christmas, Ramadan, Id ul Fitr, Passover etc, could also be included.

Older children could really go to town and try to find something special about every day! There are all the various saints' days, American Independence Day, Ground Hog Day, Armistice Day – the possibilities are endless. The project could have a religious or historical bias or be completely open-ended.

Follow-up
Once the material has been collected, be it in a book or on tape, it could be used as a focal point for assemblies.

Going to bed
(see also page 98)

Objective
To develop a project on 'sleep'.

Level of development
Seven- to eleven-year-olds.

Classroom organisation
This selection of nonsense rhymes could act as a starter for a major project on sleep. Use the verses as a basis for discussion about different aspects of sleep. Jot down key points as the discussion progresses. There are many different areas which could be explored: sleep and health; hibernation; lullabies; beds, bedclothes and nightwear through the ages; different sleeping patterns in humans and animals; myths and fables about sleep (eg Rip Van Winkle, Sleeping Beauty); sleeping potions and spells etc. The children can then choose which topic they would like to concentrate on, working either in groups or individually.

Follow-up
The project on sleep could be extended to involve the whole school. The youngest children might concentrate on learning and singing lullabies from different parts of the world; the older classes could each choose one aspect to explore.

Children can collect weather sayings from children and adults around the school.

People

Dan, Dan dirty old man
Washed his face in the frying pan
Combed his hair
With the leg of a chair
Dan, Dan dirty old man.

Eaper Weaper Chimbley Sweeper
Had a wife but couldn't keep her
Had another, didn't love her
Up the chimbley he did shove her.

Hannah Bantry
In the pantry
Gnawing at a mutton bone
How she gnawed it
How she clawed it
When she thought she was alone.

Mrs White had a fright
In the middle of the night
Saw a ghost eating toast
Half-way up a lamppost.

Three little ghostesses
Sitting on postesses
Eating buttered toastesses
Greasing their wristesses
Up to their fistesses
Oh what beastesses
To make such feastesses.

Jeremiah Obadiah, puff, puff, puff,
When he gives his message he snuffs, snuffs, snuffs,
When he goes to school by day he roars, roars, roars,
When he goes to bed at night he snores, snores,
  snores,
When he goes to Christmas treat he eats plum duff,
Jeremiah Obadiah, puff, puff, puff.

The man with nought

There was a man and he had nought
And robbers came to rob him
They crept up to the chimney pot
And then they thought they had him.

But he got down on the other side
And then they could not find him
He ran fourteen miles in fifteen days
And never looked behind him.

The milkman

Milkman, milkman, where have you been
In Buttermilk Channel up to my chin
I split my milk, and I spoilt my clothes
And got a long icicle hung from my nose.

Adam and Eve

Adam and Eve and Pinch Me
Went down to the river to bathe
Adam and Eve were drowned
Who do you think was saved?

Moses supposes

Moses supposes his toeses are roses
But Moses supposes erroneously
For nobody's toeses are posies of roses
As Moses supposes his toeses to be.

Animals

Little fly upon the wall
Ain't you got no clothes at all?
Ain't you got no shimmy shirt?
Lummy, ain't you cold?

Bat, bat come under my hat
And I'll give you a slice of bacon
And then when I bake, I'll make you a cake
If I am not mistaken.

Diddlety, diddlety, dumpty
The cat's run up the plum tree
Half a crown to get her down
Diddlety, diddlety, dumpty.

Hoddley, poddley, puddle and fogs
Cats are to marry the poodle dogs
Cats in blue jackets and dogs in blue hats
What will become of the mice and the rats?

Hickery dickery dare
The pig flew up in the air
The man in brown
Soon brought it down
Hickery dickery dare.

A young man named Cholmondley Colquhoun
Once kept as a pet a baboon
His mother said Cholmondley
Do you think it quite comely
To feed your baboon with a spoon?

The Kilkenny cats

There were once two cats of Kilkenny
Each thought there was one cat too many
So they fought and they fit
And they scratched and they bit
Till excepting their nails
And the tips of their tails
Instead of two cats there weren't any.

The language of nonsense rhymes is often rude as it has been developed by children, for children.

Mary had a little lamb
Its feet were black as soot
And into Mary's bread and jam
Its sooty foot it put.

One two three, Mother caught a flea
She put it in the teapot
And made a cup of tea
The flea jumped out
Mother gave a shout
In came Dad
With his shirt hanging out.

Piggy on the railway picking up stones
Along came an engine and broke Piggy's bones
'Oi,' said the Piggy, 'that's not fair.'
'Pooh,' said the engine driver, 'I don't care.'

The weather
(for discussion see page 94)

It's raining, it's pouring
The old man's snoring
He bumped his head
On the back of the bed
And couldn't get up in the morning.

Rain, rain go to Spain
Never come back to . . . again.
(*Insert local place name*)

Rain, rain go away
Come again another day.

Rain on the ocean, rain on the sea
Rain on the hilltops, but don't rain on me.

Whether the weather be cold
Or whether the weather be hot
We'll weather the weather
Whatever the weather
Whether we like it or not.

Seasons

The north wind doth blow
And we shall have snow
And what will the robin do then, poor thing?
He'll sit in the barn and keep himself warm
And tuck his head under his wing, poor thing.

Spring is sprung
The grass is riz
I wonder where the birdie is
They say the bird is on the wing
But that's absurd
The wing is on the bird.

Special days
(for discussion see page 95)

Christmas

Christmas is coming
The geese are getting fat
Please to put a penny in the old man's hat
If you haven't got a penny
A ha'penny will do
If you haven't got a ha'penny
God bless you.

Pancake Day

Mix the pancake
Stir the pancake
Pop it in the pan
Cook the pancake
Toss the pancake
Catch it if you can.

Mummy made pancakes on Tuesday
She tossed them in the air
One fell on the cooker
And one fell on the chair
Lucky for me, I had three
Because they fell on my plate.

Season rhymes can be used to promote artwork.

Going to bed

(for discussion see page 95)

Good night, sleep tight
Don't let the bed bugs bite
If they do, squeeze them tight.

Good night, sweet repose
Half the bed and all the clothes.

To bed, to bed says Sleepy Head
Tarry a while says Slow
Put on the pan says Greedy Nan
Let's sup before we go.

Early to bed
Early to rise
Makes a man
Healthy, wealthy and wise.

Go to bed early
Grow very tall
Go to bed late
Stay very small.

Pot luck

The sausage is a cunning bird
With feathers long and wavy
It swims about in the frying pan
And makes its nest in gravy.

If all the world were paper
And all the seas were ink
And all the trees were bread and cheese
What would we have to drink?

Humpty Dumpty sat on a wall
Eating green bananas
Where do you think he put the skins?
Down the King's pyjamas.

Humpty Dumpty sat on a wall
Humpty Dumpty had a great fall
All the King's horses and all the King's men
Said 'Scrambled eggs for dinner again!'

Tongue twisters

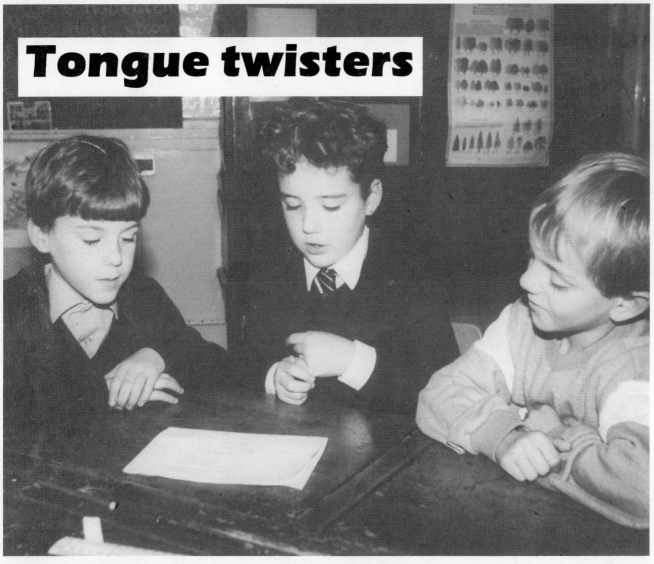

Objective

To build up a class collection of tongue twisters for possible performance.

Level of development

Seven- to eleven-year-olds.

Classroom organisation

Read, tape or write up some tongue twisters for the class. Encourage the children to have a go at mastering them. Speed and accuracy are both important. Let the children test each other, saying a tongue twister five times rapidly in succession, then ten times

etc. See if they can add any others and so build up a class collection. Parents and grandparents may be able to help.

Encourage the children to try to work out which particular combinations of sounds are difficult to reproduce at speed. They could then go on to make up their own versions.

Follow-up

The children could make an illustrated book of tongue twisters to share with other classes. Alternatively they could make a 'Tongue twister tape'. Perhaps the tongue twisters could become part of an end of term concert or show, with the audience divided into two teams to see which is best at mastering the tongue twisters, with children acting as team leaders and Master of Ceremonies. Each class might like to find a champion tongue twister reciter to compete against other classes or schools.

Red leather, yellow leather.

The Leith police dismisseth us.

Three grey geese in a green field grazing.

Around the rugged rocks, the ragged rascal ran.

Sister Susie's sewing shirts for sailors.

How much wood would a woodchuck chuck
If a woodchuck could chuck wood?

Peter Piper picked a peck of pickled peppers
A peck of pickled peppers Peter Piper picked
If Peter Piper picked a peck of pickled peppers
Where's the peck of pickled peppers Peter Piper
    picked?

She sells sea shells by the sea-shore
The shells that she sells are sea shells I'm sure
So if she sells sea shells by the sea-shore
I'm sure that the shells are sea-shore shells.

Betty Botter bought some butter
But, she said, my butter's bitter
If I put it in my batter
It will make my batter bitter
So she bought a bit of butter
Better than her bitter butter
And she put it in her batter
And it made her batter better.

Swan swam over the sea
Swim swan swim
Swan swam back again
Well swum swan.

I saw Esau sawing wood
And Esau saw I saw him.

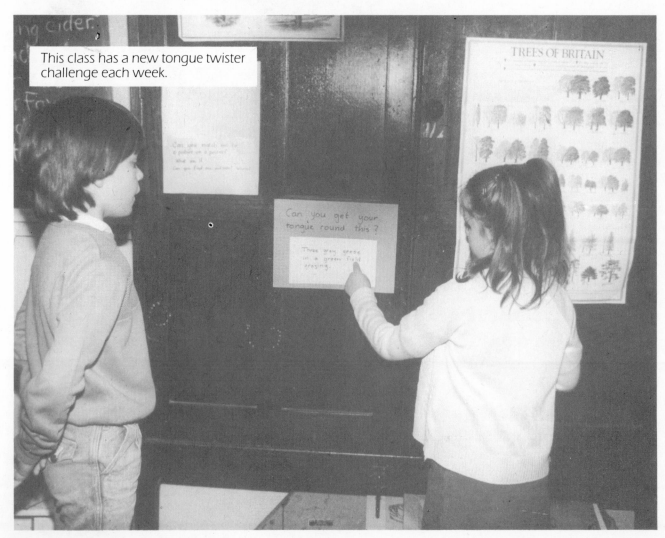

This class has a new tongue twister challenge each week.

Dips

Objective

To build up a class collection of playground 'lore'.

Level of development

Seven- to eleven-year-olds.

Classroom organisation

Use the 'dips' and playground sayings (see following section) as a starter for a discussion of playground 'lore'. Encourage the children to describe their favourites and if possible have a copy of the Opie's *Lore and Language of Schoolchildren* to look up alternative versions. You could tell the children the dips and sayings you used at school (if you can remember them!). Ask them to see if their parents/grandparents can remember their dips and rhymes and if so, to either learn them or write them down and bring them to school so that the class

can build up their own collection, either as an illustrated book or on tape.

Older children could use a tape recorder to interview other classes, other members of staff, dinner ladies etc to see if they would like to make a contribution.

Follow-up

The class book or tape could be swapped with another school, preferably one in a different area as regional variations give added interest, plus an insight into dialect.

One potato, two potato, three potato, four
five potato, six potato, seven potato more.

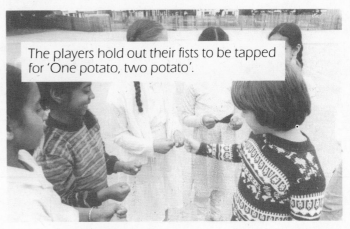

The players hold out their fists to be tapped for 'One potato, two potato'.

The children stand in a circle with both fists clenched in front of them. The person who is dipping counts the clenched fists with her own. On 'more', the person whose fist is touched puts that hand behind his back and so on until the last person left in is 'IT'.

Ip, dip, sky blue
Who's It, not you
Not because you're dirty
Not because you're clean
My mother says you're the fairy queen
So out you must go.

I lit a match
and it went OUT!

As I was walking round the lake
I met a little rattlesnake
I gave him so much jelly cake
It made his little belly ache
One, two, three
Out goes she (*or he*).

Did you ever tell a lie?
No.
Yes, you did, you know you did,
You stole my mother's teapot lid.
What colour was it?
(*Insert colour*)
No it wasn't, it was gold
That's another lie you've told
So out you must go.

Eenery, meenery minery mo
Tickle your tummy and tickle your toe
If you laugh then out you go
And that means YOU.

Eeny meeny miny maw
Erracle terracle tiny taw
One two three
Out goes she (*or he*).

Hickery dickery six and seven
Alabone crackabone ten and eleven
Spin span muskidan
Twiddle'um twaddle'um twenty-one
O-U-T spells out.

Inky pinky ponky
Daddy bought a donkey
The donkey died
Daddy cried
Inky pinky ponky.

Ibble obble
Black bobble
Ibble obble
Out
Turn a dirty dishcloth inside out
You are not IT.

Ink pink bottle of ink
You are out because you stink.

Dip dip dip
My blue ship
Sailing on the water
Like a cup and saucer
So out you must go.

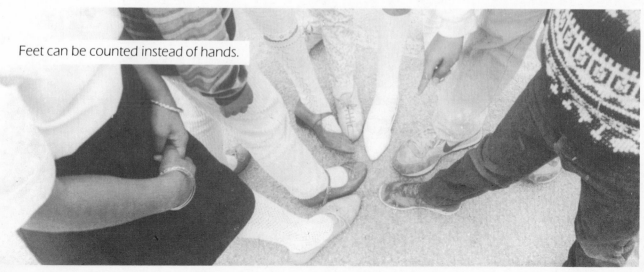

Feet can be counted instead of hands.

Ipper dipper dation
My operation
How many people at the station?
The one who comes to number . . . (*whatever*)
Will surely not be IT.

As I was walking down inky, pinky lane
I met three inky, pinky children
They asked me this and they asked me that
They asked me the colour of the Union Jack
Red, white or blue, which one are you?

Red
Red is for roses, roses, roses
Red is for roses, so out goes YOU.

White
White is for snowdrops, snowdrops, snowdrops
White is for snowdrops, so out goes YOU.

Blue
Blue is for bluebells, bluebells, bluebells
Blue is for bluebells, so out goes YOU.

Playground sayings

Objectives

To develop a project on human/animal
social rituals.

Level of development

Eight- to eleven-year-olds.

Classroom organisation

Many of the rhymes included in this section are a form of social ritual – they are used because everyone knows what they mean, both on a superficial level and on a deeper level. The children themselves may well be aware of this. Explore this idea with them using both human and animal examples such as, how do human beings behave when they meet strangers/friends/enemies? How do different animals behave? Often children enjoy a mock fight. Do young animals do the same? Certain animals (like wolves) have a clearly defined surrender posture. Is there a human equivalent? Does language help or hinder human beings? etc.

You may find it helpful to concentrate on certain basic headings: aggression, surrender, friendship, protection. Ask the children to find human and animal illustrations for each of these headings from as wide a range of sources as possible.

Shake hands, shake hands is sometimes done with both hands.

Follow-up

The information collected could be displayed visually by pictures, drawings etc and other classes/children invited to say what particular ritual was being observed. The children might like to mime or perform certain emotions, responses etc, either human or animal. This could form the basis of an assembly on feelings and responses.

Making up after a quarrel

The two children link little fingers and shake them saying:

Make up, make up
Never going to break up
If you do you'll get the cane.

or

Kiss up, kiss up
Never going to break friends
If you do you'll catch the 'flu
And that will be the end of you.

Alternatively the children shake hands and say:

Shake hands, shake hands
Never never break hands
If you do you'll get the 'flu
And that will be the end of you.

If someone is calling names

Sticks and stones may break my bones
But names will never hurt me
When I'm dead and in my grave
You'll be sorry for what you called me.

or

Same to you with brass knobs on
And buy your own Brasso to polish them.

When promising to tell the truth

Cross my heart and hope to die
If I ever tell a lie.

or

Cross my heart and hope to die
Stick a needle in my eye.

If someone is telling tales or lying

Tell tale tit
Your tongue will split
And all the little puppy dogs
Will have a little bit.

or

Liar liar, your bum's (*face's*) on fire
Your hair's sticking up like a telephone wire.

If someone is scared or a cry baby

Cowardy cowardy custard
Dipped your head in the mustard.

or

Cry Baby Bunting
Daddy's gone a hunting
Gone to fetch a rabbit's skin
To wrap Cry Baby Bunting in.

A mock threat

Stand and deliver
Your money or your liver.

A mock fight

See my finger
See my thumb
See my fist
And see it come.

If someone asks 'What's the time?'

Time you got a watch!

or

What's the time?
Half-past nine
Hang your knickers on the line
When the policeman comes along
Take them off and put them on.

When it's someone's birthday

Happy Birthday to you
Squashed tomatoes and stew
I saw a big gorilla
And it looked just like you!

On the first day of the month

Pinch, punch, first day of the month
White rabbits and no returns of any kind.

Should you forget to add 'no returns of any kind' the reply would be:

A punch and a kick
For being so quick.

or

A pinch and a blow
For being so slow.

On the subject of school dinners
(to the tune of 'Frère Jacques')

School dinners, school dinners
Concrete chips, concrete chips
Soggy semolina, soggy semolina
I feel sick
Toilet quick
It's too late
Done it on my plate.

or (to the tune of 'Sixteen tons')

If you have school dinners better push them aside
A lot of kids didn't and a lot of kids died
Potatoes of iron, carrots of steel
If the dinners don't get you then the afters will.

or (for boarders to the tune of 'There is a happy land')

There is a happy land
Far far away
Where we get poisoned
Three times a day
Bread and butter we don't see
We get sawdust in our tea
That is why we gradually
Fade, fade away.

On the last day of term

One more day of woe
One more day of sorrow
One more day in this old dump
And we'll be free tomorrow.

or (to the tune of 'Clementine')

Build a bonfire, build a bonfire
Put the teachers on the top
Put the prefects round the bottom
And we'll burn the bloomin' lot.

An ode to the teacher

My teacher's got a bunion
A face like a pickled onion
A face like a squashed tomato
And legs like string beans.

When someone asks for silence

Silence in the court
The monkey wants to talk.

or

Don't even squeak
The monkey wants to speak.

or

Silence reigned
And we all got wet.

When someone answers 'Don't care'

Don't care was made to care
Don't care was hung
Don't care was put in a pot
And boiled 'til he was done.

If someone finds something

Finders keepers
Losers weepers.

If someone is staring or copying

Copy cat, copy cat
Who do you think you're looking at?

or

Copy cat, copy cat
Sitting on the door mat.

or

I made you look, I made you stare
I made the barber cut your hair
He cut it long, he cut it short
He cut it with a knife and fork.

When choosing roles in games

Turn round
Touch the ground
Bagsee on it (or 'not it').

Shaking hands can also be done with three children.

Playground songs and jingles

Objective

To collect alternative versions of well-known songs and/or write a school song.

Level of development

Eight- to eleven-year-olds.

Classroom organisation

The children might like to collect alternative versions of well-known songs. They will probably already be familiar with some of the 'alternative' versions of carols like 'We three kings', 'While shepherds watched their flocks by night'. Other alternative versions are 'Humpty Dumpty' on page 98, 'I love a sausage' and 'Oh Jemima' on page 108.

The 'School song' (see page 108) could be used to spark off some creative lyric writing. The version given here seems to be in common use throughout the United Kingdom. Sing or play it to the class to see if they recognise it. The children may volunteer their own song which they sing on coach trips etc. If they don't have a song, see if they would like to write one! This isn't as difficult as it sounds if they write new words to a familiar tune. If they need inspiration try playing a school song you know – the ubiquitous Eton Boating Song or perhaps a funny fictional song like the one in chapter two of Jill Murphy's *The Worst Witch*.

Follow-up

The children could write, tape or perform an 'alternative' song book, either for other classes or as part of an end-of-term celebration.

You could have a competition to write a school song. If one of your staff is particularly musical she could write a tune, or else a tune could be chosen and the children write new words.

The worm song

Nobody loves me
Everybody hates me
I think I'll go and eat worms
Long thin slimy ones
Short fat fuzzy ones
Gooey gooey gooey gooey worms
Long thin slimy ones
Slip down easily
Short fat fuzzy ones stick
Short fat fuzzy ones
Stick in your throat
And the juice goes schlick, schlick, schlick.

My daddy is a dentist

My daddy is a dentist – aah, aah, aah, aah
(*For 'aah' open the mouth and point to the teeth*)
My mummy is a baker – yummy, yummy, yummy,
   yummy
(*Rub stomach with one hand*)
My sister is a show-off – honky conky, honky conky
(*On 'honky conky' one hand on hips, one hand behind head and wiggle the hips*)
My brother is a cowboy – turn around, touch the
   ground, piao, piao
(*Follow actions and on 'piao' pretend to fire*)

My mummy told me

(This song is also often used as a clapping or skipping rhyme see page 75.)

My mummy told me
If I was goody
That she would buy me
A rubber dolly
My aunty told her
I kissed a soldier
Now she won't buy me
A rubber dolly.

I love a sausage

(to the tune of 'I love a lasssie')

I love a sausage, a bonny, bonny sausage
I put one in the oven for my tea
I went down to the cellar
To fetch the salt and pepper
And the sausage ran after me.

Oh Jemima

Oh Jemima, look at your uncle Jim
He's in the duck pond learning how to swim
First he does the backstroke, then he does the side
Now he's under the water swimming against the
   tide.

Where will we be in a hundred years from now?

(sung to the tune of the 'Dead March')

They put you in a big black box
They cover you up with stones and rocks

Chorus:
Oh where will we be in a hundred years from now?

Your eyes fall in and your teeth fall out
Your brains come trickling down your snout.

Chorus

Your flesh goes all of a sickly green
The pus comes out like Devonshire cream.

Chorus

The worms crawl in and the worms crawl out
They go in thin but they come out stout.

Chorus

School song

Everywhere we go, everywhere we go
People always ask us, people always ask us
Who we are, who we are
And where we come from and where we come from
So we tell them, so we tell them
We're from . . ., we're from . . . (*insert name of school*)
The mighty . . ., the mighty . . .
And if you can't hear us, and if you can't hear us
We'll sing a little louder, we'll sing a little louder.

The verse is then repeated very loudly with the last line changing to:

And if you can't hear us, and if you can't hear us
YOU MUST BE DEAF!

A never ending story

It was a dark and stormy night
And the captain said to his mate:
'Mate, tell us a story'
And this is how the story began.
It was a dark and stormy night
and the Captain said to his mate:
'Mate, tell us a story'
And this is how the story began . . . (and so on).

You remind me of a man

You remind me of a man
What man?
The man with the power
What power?
The power of the voodoo
Who do?
You do
Do what?
Remind me of a man
What man?
The man with the power etc.

I went up one flight of stairs

I went up one flight of stairs
Just like me
I went up two flights of stairs
Just like me
I went up three flights of stairs
Just like me
I went up four flights of stairs
Just like me
I looked through the window
Just like me
I saw a monkey.
Just like me!

In a dark, dark wood

In a dark, dark wood there was a dark, dark, house
And in that dark, dark house there was a dark, dark
   room
And in that dark, dark room there was a dark, dark
   cupboard
And in that dark, dark cupboard there was a dark,
   dark shelf
And on that dark, dark shelf, there was a dark, dark
   box
And in that dark, dark box there was a GHOST!

When Susie was a baby

When Susie was a baby, a baby Susie was
She went a gaa, gaa, gaa, gaa, gaa
Gaa, gaa, gaa, gaa, gaa, gaa, gaa
(On 'gaa', the players pretend to put alternate thumbs
into their mouths)

When Susie was a schoolgirl, a schoolgirl Susie was
She went a Miss, Miss, want to do a piss
I don't know where the toilet is
(On 'Miss', the players put up their hands as though
asking for permission to talk)

When Susie was a mother, a mother Susie was
She went a rock, rock etc.
(On 'rock', players cradle an imaginary baby in their
arms and rock it)

When Susie was a granny, a granny Susie was
She went a knit, knit, lost my stitch
A knit, knit, knit etc.
(On 'knit', the players pretend to knit)

When Susie was a skeleton, a skeleton Susie was
She went a wibble wobble, wibble wobble etc.
(On 'wibble wobble' the players jerk like a skeleton)

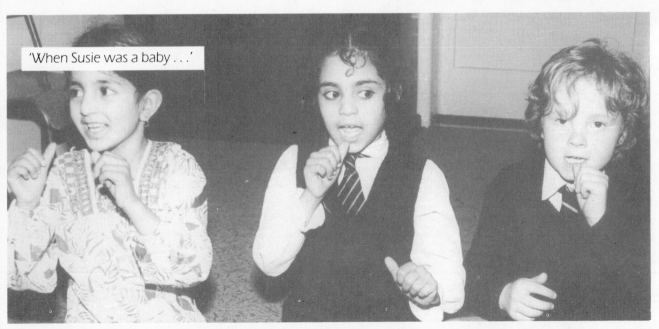
'When Susie was a baby . . .'

Resources

Nonsense rhymes compiled by Peggy Blakeley, A & C Black (1978)

The Lore and Language of School Children Iona and Peter Opie, Oxford University Press (1959)

Inky Pinky Ponky: collected playground rhymes Michael Rosen and Susanna Steele, Granada (1982)

Singing and dancing games

Singing and dancing games

INTRODUCTION

Leonora Davies has had many years of teaching experience at all levels of education from infants to higher education. She is presently music co-ordinator with the ILEA; working alongside teachers in the classroom, setting up in-service activities and generally co-ordinating music-making events. Her publications include *Sound Waves* published by Bell & Hyman and the *Primary Music Course* published by Oxford University Press. She is a frequent contributor of both articles and songs to *Child* and *Junior Education* and has also produced and compiled many resource cassettes for Scholastic Publications.

Almost all young children display an inherent responsiveness to both rhythm and melody. The fundamental concepts of movement and music are for the young child inextricably linked. Anyone who works alongside young children will appreciate that, as they sing or listen to music, their natural response is to move and to dance. The movement and dance activities in turn complement the skills involved in learning the songs, thus encouraging children to use and manipulate language.

Playground songs and chants (see page 81) provide children with a natural untutored outlet for much of their delight and exuberance. They are important not only for the glimpses they give us into the child's own understanding and perception of the world but also because they provide a natural starting point for many of the organised singing and dancing games used in a more formal way within the curriculum.

One of our roles, as teachers is to recognise children's natural uninhibited spontaneity and help children themselves to develop an understanding and awareness of it without losing their fundamental creative responsiveness. In any creative area of the curriculum there is a fine balance for the teacher, particularly with young children, between allowing children space and time to develop their own creative and imaginative ideas and in feeding in other ideas and resources which will both enrich the child's own creative vocabulary and help him to develop other skills.

Singing and dancing games offer just such a framework. A great deal of the material suggested here will help children to develop their co-ordination and motor skills as well as offering enough freedom and scope for some individual creative experimentation.

Although from a very young age children are used to dancing within a set structure, albeit very simple (for example Ring-a-ring-a-roses), they also must be given many opportunities to dance individually and in unstructured situations. For instance children need to be able to practise and acquire body control with skipping and stepping freely before they can skip to eight counts, stop, turn and skip back. It is very important that teachers are aware of these stages of development.

Some of the games suggested here begin by simply helping children to use and develop stepping, running, hopping and skipping activities and these are done quite freely. In all these singing and dancing activities the main emphasis is on the combination of the language, the music and movement. By starting at an early age children's natural, uninhibited responses to the music will combine gradually with greater physical control and co-ordination. Some of the examples suggested are not specifically singing or dancing games but are songs that have dance possibilities. It is hoped that teachers may be able to use these examples as a guide and framework for choosing their own material and developing their own and the children's ideas in similar ways.

The physical interpretation of pulse and beat and melodic phrasing are important and valuable ways of developing and re-inforcing the basic musical concepts. In preparing material of this kind it is important to look beyond the actual song or dance. It will be necessary sometimes to extract a musical or physical idea or concept and develop it or work on it in a variety of ways during the lesson before re-inserting it in its original context. This way of working may help the child to focus on a particular idea and understand it more clearly than when it is surrounded by many others.

The basic element underlying most of these singing and dancing games is the *pulse* beat. Children need to practise feeling and experiencing the pulse in a variety of ways. Before beginning any dancing, let them respond to the music by clapping, swaying or dancing individually. This can be done with even the youngest children. Suggestions for specific activities which will help children to develop, to build on and to reinforce their experiences in this work can be found in the 'General advice' section. This work will help the children when they come to the more complex line and circle formations.

Encourage children to develop their own lyrics and movements.

Often the success of more formal dances appears to depend on the children's ability to count steps. By encouraging them to listen and respond to the musical phrases, they will begin to acquire an overall concept of the dance, instead of seeing it as a counting exercise.

Some of the material is developed to include specific suggestions and links for instrumental involvement. Many of these ideas can be and should be followed up and developed in music area activities. In some cases particular musical skills will need to be worked on in a music session before returning to combine them with the movement and dance skills. Some of the later more developed activities will give older children an opportunity to choose whether they wish to dance or play for the dance.

General advice

Learning the songs

Most of the melodies for these singing games are simple enough to be learned and absorbed by the children at the same time as they move or dance. It could be that the children stand still briefly whilst they listen to the tune and the words once or twice, but the combination of the movement with the singing should be experienced as early in the learning process as possible. The 'skill' from one discipline will complement the other. However, some of the singing games that are particularly suitable for the older children, may need to be taught as songs initially before combining them with the dance suggestions, though these too should be combined as soon as possible.

It may be a good idea to have some children providing the singing whilst the others dance to begin with, making sure that they change over so that everyone has a turn to do both disciplines.

Accompaniments

Most of these songs should be sung unaccompanied. This enables the teacher to take an active part in the movement and dance. This is particularly important with younger children. Guitar or auto-harp will also be effective and in very few cases simple piano accompaniments have been suggested. In these cases it would be advisable to have at least two adults available.

Apart from the few instances where instrumental accompaniments have been suggested, teachers and pupils can pitch their own starting notes. Always make sure that the children are quite clear what the starting note is. It is advisable with the older children to 'hum' or 'lah' this note before starting. With younger children they usually 'pitch' into your starting note as you start to sing. If you are using an accompaniment then the song should be sung in the key and at the pitch suggested. Use the patterns to provide a simple introduction. This will also help children to pitch the starting note.

A guitar is an effective accompaniment to many songs.

Pulse, beat and rhythm activities

As the children's responses to music and dance develop they should begin to be able to group the beats into patterns of 2, 3, 4 and even 5 and 7. The following basic activities will help them to begin to 'feel' the beat. They can be worked through with quite young children though the older children will respond with a greater degree of 'accuracy'.

Count a steady pattern of

1 2 3 4 1 2 3 4 1 2 3 4

Add some body sounds to the counting:

```
1  2  3  4  1  2  3  4  1  2  3  4
X  –  –  –  X  –  –  –  X  –  –  –
```

Emphasise the first beat in each group with a different sound to the others. Add some movements to these:

```
1         2         3    4    1  2  3  4
X         tap       tap  tap  X  –  –  –
clap      shoulders
```
or

```
1         2     3     4     1  2  3  4
X         step  step  step  X  –  –  –
knee
bend
```

Try this kind of activity using other groupings:

```
1         2     3     1  2  3  1  2  3
X         –     –     X  –  –  X  –  –
knee      clap  clap
slap
```

To begin with encourage the children to count the patterns out loud. Later they will be able to count these 'in their heads' and add the movements and body sounds.

117

Teaching about gaps

With the class standing in a circle, choose one child to set up a simple pattern – two claps followed by two gaps, indicated by an open hand gesture – on a steady count of:

1– 2– 1– 2– 1– 2– 1– 2
X X – – X X – –

Let everyone join in to keep it going. Decide which way round the circle the game will proceed.

The first child begins and says her name into the first gap. The next child says his name into the next gap.

The game proceeds round the circle with everyone in turn putting their names in the gaps while maintaining the clapping.

Keep the pulse pattern steady and even throughout. Children unable to find one gap may be able to find the next one. Although this activity appears to be quite straightforward it is advisable to work through it before going on to the other variations. The names should be said in the normal spoken way.

Check your pulse

Let one child choose a pattern of steady beats and decide on a suitable speed, for example:
patterns of 3 – moderately fast
patterns of 4 – fast
patterns of 2 – slowly.

Clap the pattern of beats, stressing the first beat in each pattern, for example:

1–2–3, 1–2–3, 1–2–3, or
1–2–3–4, 1–2–3–4, 1–2–3–4.

The rest of the class can join in when they are ready. Repeat the activity, choosing different patterns of beats and different speeds.

Take care to keep the pattern of beats even to maintain the chosen speed (do not slow down or speed up). It may help to count the chosen pattern out loud to begin with.

Many of these pulse-based activities using body sounds can be reinforced and developed by transferring these ideas to the music area. For example, the above game can be played using instruments instead of clapping.

Further suggestions and activities for developing the material given here musically can be found in *Sound Waves* (see Resources on page 172).

Who is in the middle?

Many circle games require one child to start the activity in the centre. In order to select who will go into the middle in an unbiased way you can play a simple preliminary game. It is important for children to feel that it is not always the teacher who chooses who this might be. Young children particularly are much happier if this selection process has been done at 'random' even though the activity may take a little longer. Choose any simple song or chant. As the children sing, they pass a drum round the circle. Whoever is holding the drum when the song ends will go into the centre. Repeat this as many times as you need to select the number of children you require.

Organising the music area

A music area is a vital extension to the song and dance lesson. Children need time to explore and develop their ideas in their own time and many of the dancing and singing games here suggest ways in which this can be done. A small table or 'area' should be set

Let one child choose a clapping rhythm for the rest of the class to join in.

aside in the classroom for children to work in this way. Class teachers must devise their own 'rules' and if necessary their own 'restrictions' on the use of this area. It is important that the work done in the music area is valued and shared with the other children. If the classroom structure is flexible this can be done at the time or may be more appropriately shared at a special time set aside for 'music area' presentations.

Clap your hands

Objectives

A very basic movement game which encourages children to keep in time to a specific beat and rhythm. Both children and teachers can extend this in any way that seems appropriate.

Level of development

Four- to five-year-olds.

Classroom organisation

In the initial stages of teaching the song, you will need to demonstrate where the actions occur. To begin with very young children will want to clap all the time. With a firm leadership the children will soon realise where the clapping etc should happen. Choose other actions that the children can do easily, for example 'Click your fingers', 'Slap your knees', 'Tap your toes', 'Stamp your feet' etc. (Some young children find clicking fingers quite difficult.)

Follow-up

Encourage the children to take the lead. Develop this to other movements or actions ie tie your laces/wash your face/smile like me etc.

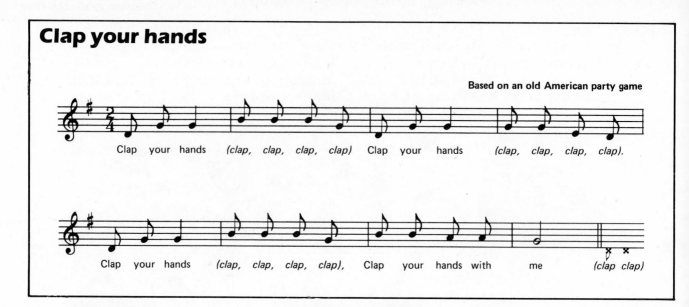

Clap your hands

Based on an old American party game

Clap your hands (clap, clap, clap, clap) Clap your hands (clap, clap, clap, clap).

Clap your hands (clap, clap, clap, clap), Clap your hands with me (clap clap)

Tidey oh

Objectives

This singing game can be as simple or as complex as your pupils can cope with. It offers a great deal of scope for improvisation and the introduction of a wide variety of musical ideas. It can be sung loud/quiet, slow/fast etc. The verses can be altered to include different actions or a combination of two or even three actions. Once the children are confident with the framework you can encourage them to make suggestions for new verses.

Level of development

Five- to seven-year-olds.

Classroom organisation

Use the first verse to introduce the tune and allow the children time to gain their confidence. On the chorus everyone jingles their hands above their heads and wiggles from side to side. Each verse thereafter should be completely self explanatory. Try to vary the verses so that some involve moving around the space in a particular way ('Creep around tidey oh') and some suggest more static movements ('Tap your knees tidey oh'). You can introduce different musical concepts, eg 'Sing very loud tidey oh' or 'Clap very slowly tidey oh'. Another alternative is to have a combination of movements, eg 'Put one finger on your head, put one finger on your nose, put two fingers on your knees, Jingle at the windows tidey oh'.

Tidey oh

Skip one win-dow, ti-dey oh, Skip two win-dows, ti-dey oh,

Skip three win-dows, ti-dey oh, Jin-gle at the win-dows, ti-dey oh,

Chorus
Jing-ling, jing-ling, jing-ling Jo, Jin-gle at the win-dows, ti-dey oh.

Skip one window, tidey oh,
Skip two windows, tidey oh,
Skip three windows, tidey oh,
Jingle at the windows, tidey oh.

Chorus:
Jingling, jingling, jingling jo,
Jingle at the windows, tidey oh.

Put your fingers on your head . . .
(*Chorus*)

Put your fingers on your nose . . .

(*Chorus*)

Put your fingers on your knees . . .
(*Chorus*)

Tap your toes up and down . . .
(*Chorus*)

Put one finger on your head,
Put one finger on your nose,
Put your fingers on your knees,
Jingle at the windows, tidey oh.
(*Chorus*)

Sur le pont

Objectives

A simple singing/dancing game based on a popular traditional French folk tune. The original has slightly out-dated overtones but it can be adapted in a variety of ways to involve individual and original ideas.

Level of development

Five- to seven-year-olds.

Classroom organisation

This is a circle game but the children will need to be numbered off in 'two's'. For the chorus the children hold hands and dance round in a circle. For the first verse the boys 'bow' as they sing 'this way' and the girls curtsy as they sing 'The ladies they go this way.'

Additional verses could encourage the children to make up a movement or a dance step as they sing the first line. Their partners copy the movement as they sing the response line. For example, 'I'm going to dance like this now' – points toes to the left then the right. The partner sings and replies doing the same step. Or you could encourage the children to do something quite different from their partner.

Follow-up

The leader (this would not necessitate the need to number off in boy/girl pairings but simply in pairs, which is really preferable) claps a rhythm pattern as they sing. 'I'm going to clap this now' and the partner replies with same or different pattern. This can lead directly to doing the same activity with musical instruments. One child plays a pattern. Her partner echoes the same pattern back on her instrument. You could develop this work further to involve much longer 'musical conversations'.

Sur le pont

Traditional French folk tune

On the bridge at A-vi-gnon they are danc-ing, they are
Sur le pont d'A-vi-gnon l'on y dan-se, l'on y

danc-ing, On the bridge at A-vi-gnon they are danc-ing in a ring.
dan-se, Sur le pont d'A-vi-gnon l'on y dan-se tout en rond.

The gen-tle-men go this way, Then a-gain go this way.
Les beaux mes-sieurs font comm' ça. Et puis en-cor' comm' ça.

Look at the fish

Objectives

This is a singing game in which the children are encouraged to take an active singing role by responding to a group or teacher-led verse with a short melodic phrase. At the same time it can involve some simple individual movement responses.

123

Level of development

Five- to seven-year-olds.

Classroom organisation

Sing the verse with the children. Then the teacher/leader looks at one child and sings 'Hey little fish . . .' The child replies 'my name is . . .' and inserts his name. If movement is possible he then comes out to the front of the class to 'swim around' as a spiky or fat (or any other shape) fish. Continue singing until a number of fish are at the front of the class. Encourage each child to make a different shape as they move.

Encourage the children to make different shaped fish with their bodies.

Follow-up

The children can make up their own verses about other shaped or coloured fish. This song links well with art or topic work.

Look at the fish

Words and music by Leonora Davies

Look at the fish swim-ming there___ In the deep blue sea.

Spi-ky and fat ones, short and flat ones, Some I can hard-ly see.

Hey lit-tle fish now what's your name?___ Won't you say hel-lo to me.

My ___ name is Mary ___ and I live in the deep blue sea.
Jonathon
Bill
Saleem

Dance in a circle

Objectives

This is an American folk song which can be adapted and developed in various ways. A wide variety of musical ideas – speeds, dynamics (loud and quiet) and different rhythmic patterns can be emphasised and reinforced through the introduction of a movement idea.

Level of development

Five- to six-year-olds.

Classroom organisation

The song and the movement can be incorporated immediately. For the chorus the children join hands and move round in a circle as they sing. For the verses the children break from the circle formation and

dance freely. Introduce new verses: 'Skip on your own . . .', 'Tip-toe on your own . . .' etc. Return to the chorus/circle to finish with.

Follow-up

Let the children choose other ways of moving and alter the rhythm of the tune appropriately. Children could focus on the different pulse changes ie from three beats for the chorus to four beats for the marching by playing these on different instruments. Encourage them even from this early age to group and accent the beats in groups:

1 2 3 4 1 2 3 4 or 1 2 3 1 2 3
X   X   X   X

Follow this up in the music area. Make a simple work card to encourage the children to play three beat patterns or four beat patterns. Let them work in pairs each playing a different instrument. See 'General advice' (page 116) for further suggestions.

125

Dance in a circle

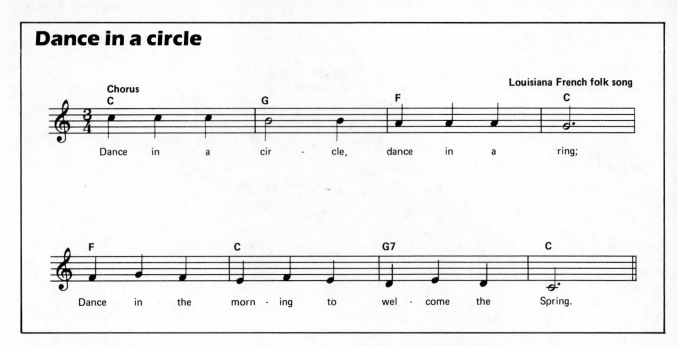

Louisiana French folk song

Chorus

Dance in a **cir** - **cle**, **dance** in a **ring**;

Dance in the **morn** - ing to **wel** - come the **Spring**.

Chorus:
Dance in a circle,
Dance in a ring;
Dance in the morning
To welcome the spring.

Dance on your own
Around and around
Dance very slowly
Now sit on the ground.

Chorus

March, skip, walk, creep etc.

Baak bakum paira (The pigeon)

Objectives

This is a simple Bengali folk song. The phonetisation means that everyone can sing the song in Bengali. An English translation might be: 'Coo pigeon, bring the wedding crown, the bride marries tomorrow, she will go on a golden cart.'

Level of development

Five- to seven-year-olds.

Classroom organisation

Teach the song and the actions together. Sing a line at a time and demonstrate the action for the children to echo back. Observe the pauses at the end of each phrase. It is particularly important when working with very young children to give them time to make the appropriate action. The actions given here are suggestions only. Your school may have teachers or parents who could demonstrate other appropriate Indian dance movements. When the children are familiar with the tune they should sing it all the way through.

Baak bakum paira – flap arms like a bird.
Matay die taira – put on the crown.
Bow shazbe kalki – palms together, move hands round in a circle.
Chorrbe shonar palki – roll hands round each other.

After singing the verse through once standing still let the children move gently round the hall making up other actions for each phrase. They could also work in small groups and try to 'dramatise' the ideas as they sing.

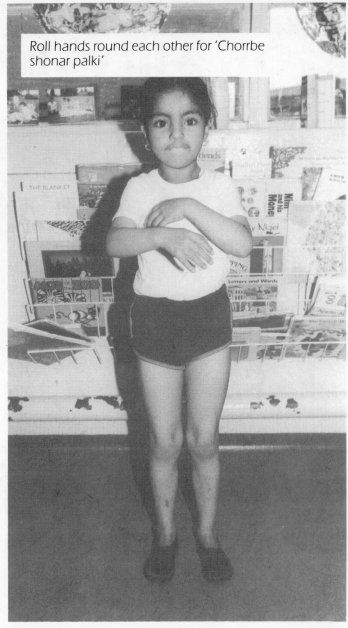

Roll hands round each other for 'Chorrbe shonar palki'

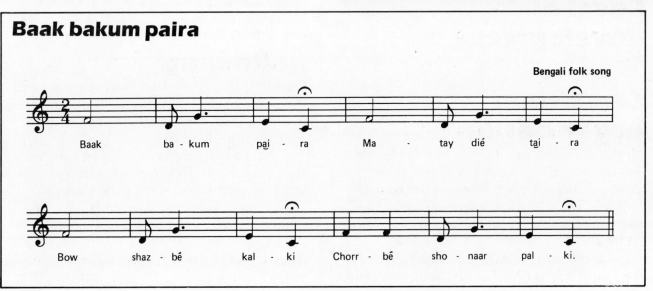

Baak bakum paira

Bengali folk song

Baak ba - kum pai - ra Ma - tay dié tai - ra

Bow shaz - bé kal - ki Chorr - bé sho - naar pal - ki.

127

Oh will you come a-sailing?

Objectives

This very simple activity offers an early experience of a more formal dancing game. The words are repetitive and easy to learn.

Level of development

Five- to seven-year-olds.

Classroom organisation

Divide the class into two lines. Line A will ask the questions, Line B will give the answers. Line A skips towards the centre singing 'Oh will you come a-sailing, a-sailing, a-sailing?' and back 'O will you come a-sailing, a-sailing o'er the sea?'

Line B does exactly the same thing as they sing 'We cannot . . . The song continues

in this way with each line skipping to the centre and out again in turn.

On the last verse 'Oh yes we'll come a dancing . . ., instead of skipping back as before, all the children in line B continue to dance towards their partners. Everyone sings the tune to 'lah' as they dance freely round the room with their partners.

Follow-up

Children in the line that is waiting can clap the pulse beat as they sing. Let the children make up their own verses for some more questions and answers.

This work can be developed directly in the music area. Children work in pairs, each with an instrument. One child plays a pattern on a woodblock and his partner answers with something quite different on the tambourine. Let the children develop a question and answer conversation in this way.

Oh will you come a-sailing?

Gaily in skipping time

Oh will you come a - sail - ing, a - sail - ing, a - sail - ing, Oh

will you come a - sail - ing, a - sail - ing o'er the sea? ____

We cannot come a-sailing, a-sailing, a-sailing,
We cannot come a-sailing, we have no ship, you see.

Oh will you come a-riding, a-riding, a-riding?
Oh will you come a-riding, a-riding o'er the lea?

We cannot come a-riding, a-riding, a-riding,
We cannot come a-riding, we have no horse you see.

Oh will you come a-fishing, a-fishing, a-fishing?
Oh will you come a-fishing in the sea?

We cannot come a-fishing, a-fishing, a-fishing,
We cannot come a-fishing, we have no nets, you see.

Oh will you come a-dancing, a-dancing, a-dancing?
Oh will you come a-dancing, a-dancing, gay and
free?

Oh yes, we'll come a-dancing, a-dancing, a-dancing,
Oh yes, we'll come a-dancing, a-dancing, gay and
free.

This song can be developed further in the
music area.

129

Manuel road

Objectives

This was originally a Jamaican 'work' song but has now become a children's game song. A number of 'work songs' from around the world can be found, each with a steady pulse beat. In this version the steady beat is kept by passing 'stones' or 'bean bags' round in a circle.

Level of development

Seven- to eleven-year-olds.

Classroom organisation

The children sit in a circle. If the class is very large divide the class into two smaller circles. Each child has a stone or bean bag. The leader/teacher sets the speed and pulse of the song. Choose a reasonable speed to begin with. The children begin by marking time with the bean bag on the first beat of

the bar. Use this idea as an introduction to the song over four bars. It will help to settle the pulse and the children will find it easier to pass the bean bags. During the chorus 'Go down Manuel road' children mark time with their bean bag on the first beat of the bar. On the verse 'Break them one by one' everyone passes their bean bag to the person on their right. (It is crucial that the children know which way round the circle to pass.) The physical movement will be: pick up on the word 'Break' and put down on the word 'one', ie on the first and third beats of the bar. Continue like this repeating 'break them one by one' over and over until someone fumbles or drops their bean bag. If a child drops his bean bag he must stand up outside the circle but continue to help keep the rhythm by clapping. The child on his right now has to pass two bean bags and everyone sings 'Break them two by two.' The game continues until the next time when everyone sings 'three by three.'

Manuel road

Chorus   Jamaican folk song

Go down Ma - nu - el road, girl and boy ___ we go break rock stone.

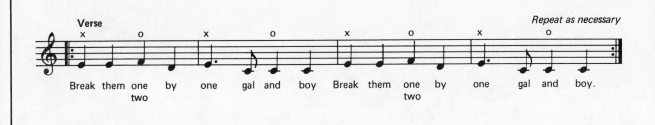

Verse   Repeat as necessary

Break them one by one gal and boy Break them one by one gal and boy.
       two   two

Children who are 'out' can continue to keep the rhythm by clapping.

Follow-up

This original intention can get quite difficult and children rarely get beyond 'three by three'. You could modify it slightly to focus on 'musical' developments rather than co-ordination skills. Each time someone drops their bean bag start singing the chorus 'Go down Manuel road' again, but establish a slightly faster speed and pulse. Do this over four bars so that the new speed and pulse are clearly established before the children begin to sing. They continue to pass *one* bean bag. The intention is to see how fast they can pass the bean bag. As before those who drop the bean bag can stand outside the circle and help to keep the pulse by clapping.

131

Pass the pebble on

Objectives

This Ghanaian singing game will help to reinforce a steady beat through physical movement.

Level of development

Seven- to eleven-year-olds.

Classroom organisation

Have the children kneel in a circle. Each child has a stone/bean bag/playing brick. Begin by singing the song through and clapping on the first and third beats of the bar. One child could emphasise this beat on a drum.

The first time round the children sing as they pass the bean bag on the first beat and swing their arms back to pick up the next one on the third beat. Encourage the children to really feel the beat as they swing their arms across their bodies as they pass the bean bags on.

The second time the child playing the drum chooses a faster speed. Play two bars before singing the song to help establish the new speed. If necessary sing the song through once at the new speed before passing the bean bags round.

Each time you sing the song establish a slightly faster speed and pulse before the singing starts. See how fast you can get before someone fumbles or drops their stone. When someone 'misses' they stand outside the circle and join in by clapping the beat with the drum player.

Ghanaian pronunciation

Mele ni yaa ee. Damoshe me shebo × 2. Ke otay yaake manche Taki ake mingbi. Ke nigbe woyaa woyaa Adabraka wuamo gbayee.

English translation

Tell the ship that is going to wait for a message. If you go, send my greetings to King Taki. I'm going to Adabraka to find a place.

132

Pass the pebble on

Ghanaian children's song

Pass the peb - ble on, / Me - le ni yaa ee — Try to keep it stead - y. / Da - mo - she me she - bo

Pass the peb - ble on, / Me - le ni yaa ee — Try to keep it stead - y / Da - mo - she me she - bo — You'll / Ke

soon be out if you don't move in time to the beat! / ot - ay yaa - ke man - che Ta - ki a - ke ming - bi — You'll / Ke

soon be out if you don't move in time to the beat! / nig - be wo - yaa wo - yaa Ada braka wua - mo gba - yee.

Bingo was his name oh!

Objectives

A simple singing game, where children

begin to internalise a rhythmic pattern by thinking the beat/word instead of singing the song.

133

Level of development

Seven- to nine-year-olds.

Classroom organisation

Children sing the song all through. They can clap the rhythm of the word BINGO as they sing each time it occurs.

The first time you sing it through leave out the letter 'O'. If the children are clapping they will find it helpful to make an 'open hand' movement at this point. This prevents them from clapping in the 'gap'. Come in again on the last phrase 'And Bingo was his name oh'. The second time leave out the 'G' and the 'O'. Proceed in this way, dropping out a letter each time until all the letters of BINGO are silent.

Follow-up

You could either have five children with instruments and the rest of the class singing or give instruments to every child in the group. If possible use five different types of instruments and divide the group into five groups.

Instead of a silent beat on each letter, you could have instruments representing the letters eg

'O' – tambourines
'G' – bells/triangles
'N' – wooden instruments
'I' – chime bars
'B' – drums.

The first time round everyone sings the song through. On the letter 'O' the tambourine group will play whilst the singing is silent.

On the second time through the bells play on the letter 'G' and the tambourines play on the letter 'O'. Proceed in this way adding a new instrument each time.

You may like to rehearse the instrument section before fitting it into the singing game. It can sound very effective once the children have absorbed the sequence. You could also have children standing up with the appropriate letters each time they occur.

Each child has to play their instrument when their letter is missed out.

Bingo was his name oh!

Somebody's knocking at your door

Objectives

This can either be used as a singing activity or as a circle game. Instruments can be introduced to provide an added focus. The musical focus is on rhythm patterns. Children will need to have done some initial work on clapping and recognising their name patterns (see page 118).

Level of development

Seven- to eleven-year-olds.

Classroom organisation

The children sit in two lines facing a partner. Line A will lead and Line B will answer. Before starting the song, work down each line to make sure that each child can clap their own name pattern. Try to encourage them to clap their name in the way that they speak it so that they are not forcing an un-natural rhythm.

All the children sing the song. At the word 'door' the first child in line A (Sam) claps his name rhythm. This is repeated. When you get to 'Oh . . . why don't you answer', all the children insert the name of the child sitting opposite Sam (Wendy). At the end of the verse Wendy will clap her name pattern in reply. The song proceeds with the next child in line A clapping for the next child in line B. Repeat the song over and over again until all the children have had a turn. For variety each child could have an instrument to play and sing their name pattern.

'Somebody is knocking at your door' can also be done as a singing/dancing game. Choose three or four children to hide behind a screen, with an instrument each. The others join hands and walk round as they sing. They stop each time at the word 'door' to listen to someone behind the screen playing the name pattern of someone in the circle. Any child who thinks that they have heard their name pattern then steps into the centre. This may well be more than one child. The children singing choose one name to sing at 'Oh . . . why don't you

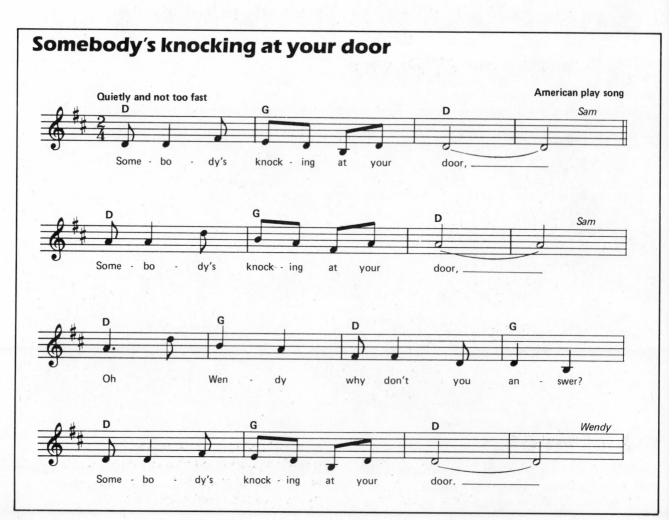

answer?' It may be that two or three
different names are sung. This will not
matter as they should all have the same
rhythmic pattern. If a child steps into the
circle who does not have this pattern to her
name, let her clap the pattern anyway to
help her begin to understand. This is
definitely not a game where it matters if
the children are incorrect.

Children will have to listen carefully to the
patterns being played.

Follow-up
Working in pairs children can make longer
rhythmic patterns by playing their name
patterns two or three times. Taking it in
turns, one child plays the rhythm that his
name makes a few times and his partner
answers with his own pattern. Later they
can see what happens if they try to fit the
two patterns together.

Round and round the island

Objectives
This is a highly adaptable singing game
which can be modified and changed to suit
your own purposes. This version involves
some simple movement and some
instrumental activity.

Round and round the island

Words by Leonora Davies

Brightly

Round and round the is - land Round and round the is - land

Round and round the is - land We march all in a line

Hush, I think I hear a sound Hush, I think I

Sing the following verses slightly slower

hear a sound Hush, I think I hear a sound

Pause

The wind blows through the trees Hum-ming bird in the tree

(Sound of leaves in the wind, the sea, humming bird)

Choruses:
Round and round the island,
Round and round the island,
Round and round the island,
We all march in line.

In and out the palm trees,
In and out the palm trees,
In and out the palm trees,
We creep on hands and knees.

Verses:
Hush, I think I hear a sound,
Hush, I think I hear a sound,
Hush, I think I hear a sound, PAUSE . . . . .
The wind blows through the trees.

Hush, I think I hear a sound,
Hush, I think I hear a sound,
Hush, I think I hear a sound, PAUSE . . . . .
The sea comes rolling in.

Hush, I think I hear a sound,
Hush, I think I hear a sound,
Hush, I think I hear a sound, PAUSE . . . . .
Humming bird in the tree.

The verses and choruses can be put into any
order.

Let the children experiment with different
ways of making the sounds.

Level of development

Six- to eight-year-olds.

Classroom organisation

Let some children play the instrumental
accompaniment sitting to one side. The rest
of the children join hands and march round
in a circle as they sing the first part of the
chorus. They then drop hands and follow
the appropriate actions for the second part.
When singing the verses they should sit and
listen carefully. In the pause, one of the
instrumental players makes their sound and
the children listening must sing whichever
it is. These verse and choruses can be put
into any order and this will encourage the
children to listen carefully.

The sounds can be made in a variety of
ways. Wind can be suggested by blowing
over the tops of bottles or using the end of a
recorder and wavering the hands around
the end. The sea sounds can be suggested
by swirling rice or pebbles around in a tray
or up-turned drum (or just vocally). The
humming bird sound can be made by
blowing through paper wrapped around a
comb.

Follow-up

When the children are familiar with the
sounds, the children playing the
instrumental parts could 'hide' behind a
screen so that the other children cannot see
which instrument is being played. This
means that the children have to listen even
more carefully. Let the children behind the
screen decide which order they will play in.
Encourage the children to think of other
sounds that they might hear on an island.
This material can be adapted to suit any
geographical location. It could be 'Round
and round the streets' or 'Round and round
the park'. Encourage the children to think of
sounds that they would hear in these
locations.

I can hear two people

Objectives

A simple singing activity which introduces the use of instruments. The musical ideas focus on getting louder then quieter and on keeping a steady pulse beat.

Level of development

Six- to eight-year-olds.

Classroom organisation

For this song each child will need an unpitched instrument: drums, tambourines, wood blocks etc.

    Teach the song initially using clapping or knee slaps to keep the left/right pattern.

Number the children off in twos. The first time two children sing 'I can hear two people'. The next time four children will sing and so on. When all the children are singing they must then drop out in twos and count backwards. The effect will be that the song gradually gets quieter. Encourage the children to sing very quietly as they finish.

    Repeat this process again but this time the children join in with their instruments, just keeping the steady pulse beat.

Follow-up

Ask the children to group in threes or fours. This could involve more children. 'I can hear three people' then 'I can hear six people' etc. Link this work to number activities.

    If the children are in a suitable space

they could sing and play as they walk about keeping the pulse beat as they go. As each pair/three/four joins in they can form a line behind each other.

This could be extended into different ways of moving: walking, running, skipping etc. This will involve the additional musical idea of speed and tempo. For example, 'I can hear two children running down the street' should be sung at a quicker tempo/speed than 'I can hear two children walking . . . .' For 'I can hear two children skipping down the street' the rhythm will need to change slightly (see music).

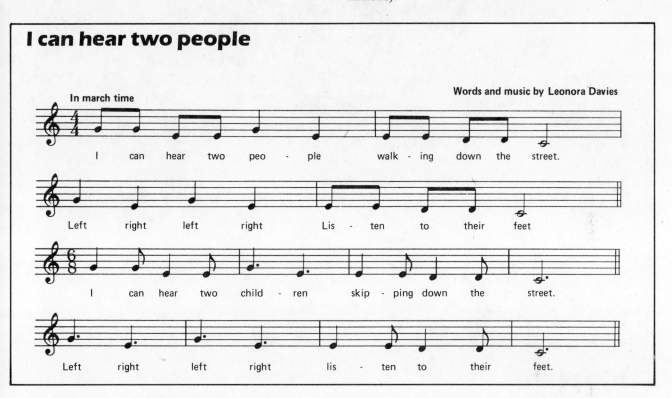

I can hear two people

In march time

Words and music by Leonora Davies

I can hear two peo - ple walk - ing down the street.

Left right left right Lis - ten to their feet

I can hear two child - ren skip - ping down the street.

Left right left right lis - ten to their feet.

This song can be extended by suggesting different ways of moving.

I'm a great big lorry

Objectives

This song incorporates musical ideas of fast and slow and introduces the idea of getting faster and slower. These ideas are reinforced with free movement ideas.

Level of development

Five- to six-year-olds.

Classroom organisation

Let the children spread out over a large space. As they sing they move around, weaving in and out of each other. Stop at the end of verse one. Proceed with the other verses with children moving in the appropriate way. Encourage the children to make up other verses about things they see and hear on the road. This could be linked with a 'listening walk' to make a list of the sounds they can hear. 'I'm a dustbin lorry, making a lot of noise, put out your rubbish, I'm coming up the road.' 'I'm a clattery milk-float, clanking down the road, how many bottles do you want today?'

Follow-up

Divide the children into three groups (for the original song). Each group chooses someone to play an instrument. The child playing the drum must 'control' the speed of the children as they move. With very young children, let them play quite freely as long as the intention of fast or slow is clear. Older children can begin to keep a steady pulse beat for the others to move to. Ropes or hoops can be used to indicate traffic lights or bus stops etc.

In the music area children can work out a simple accompaniment pattern using notes A and D. This can be added to the movement and singing. The speed of this accompaniment will need to change in order to fit with each verse.

142

I'm a great big lorry

Traditional tune, words by Leonora Davies

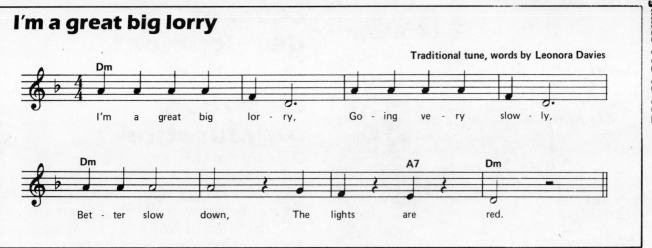

I'm a great big lor - ry, Go - ing ve - ry slow - ly,

Bet - ter slow down, The lights are red.

I'm a busy police car,
Travelling very quickly,
Listen to my siren
Don't get in my way.

I'm a big red bus,
Taking people home.
Ring my bell,
It's time to stop.

How did Jane/Ben come to school?

Objectives

A singing game with a set circle structure which also allows children to make individual responses and develop individual ideas. The musical ideas encourage keeping a steady beat both in movement, walking and clapping.

You could link the different ways of moving (walking/running/hopping etc) to the musical ideas of speed/tempo. Is it fast/slow? Does the movement or the beat get faster/slower?

143

Encourage the children to invent unusual ways in which they could have come to school.

Level of development
Five- to six-year-olds.

Classroom organisation
Choose a child to start the game off in the middle of the circle. Everyone walks round her as they sing: 'How did (name of child in the middle) come to school?' Encourage the children to step on the beat as they walk round. On the words 'Show us Jane' everyone stands still and keeps the steady pulse beat with a clap. Jane decides how she will move and demonstrates this to the others. Then everyone joins and moves about in the same way as Jane. She then chooses another child to go into the centre and the game continues.

Follow-up
Encourage the children to choose different vehicles to come to school in: cars/lorries/bus or even quite imaginary ideas such as a helicopter/the tardis/a space ship etc. All these ideas might involve further movement or drama links. Encourage the children to make the sounds to go with these methods of transport as they move about.

How did Jane come to school?

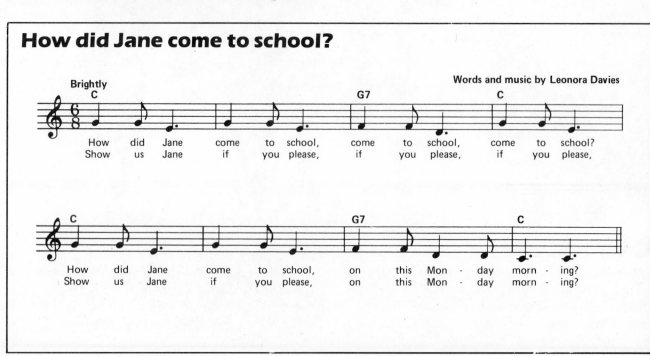

Brightly

Words and music by Leonora Davies

How did Jane come to school, come to school, come to school?
Show us Jane if you please, if you please, if you please,

How did Jane come to school, on this Mon-day morn-ing?
Show us Jane if you please, on on this Mon-day morn-ing?

Put on your shoes

Objectives

The musical focus for this singing game can range from 'timbre' (the different sound that shoes make) to dynamics (loud and quiet sounds) or speed (moving quickly or slowly). It could also involve rhythmic work – walking/running/skipping/hopping patterns.

Level of development

Six- to eight-year-olds.

Classroom organisation

Children holds hands and dance around a child standing in the centre of a circle as they sing the question 'What kind of shoes shall we put on to-day?' The children describe the shoes that the child in the middle is wearing 'Sally puts her sandals on' and then make up a sound to match the noise that her shoes make as she walks around. Alternatively, at the end of the chorus she chooses a pair of shoes to put on and the children sing about those shoes and the sound they make. This can either be left

to the individual's imagination or there could be a selection of different shoes in the centre of the circle – football boots, ballet shoes, high heels, climbing boots etc – or pictures of shoes or people wearing shoes. Whoever is in the centre must choose a pair to put on.

This could also be played sitting down. As the children sing they pass a shoe round. Pictures of various shoes are face down in a pile in the centre of the circle. The child holding the shoes at the end of the chorus chooses a card. The children then sing about the shoe selected.

Follow-up

Put four or five different pairs of shoes in the centre. The game proceeds as before but this time the sound of each shoe will also be represented by a different instrument. Let the children choose which instruments will be best suited to the sounds of the shoes in the middle. You may like to choose four or five children beforehand to play the instruments or you could pass two shoes as they sing, in opposite directions. At the end of the chorus one child will select which shoes to put on and the other will choose an instrument to play.

145

Put on your shoes

Words and music by Leonora Davies

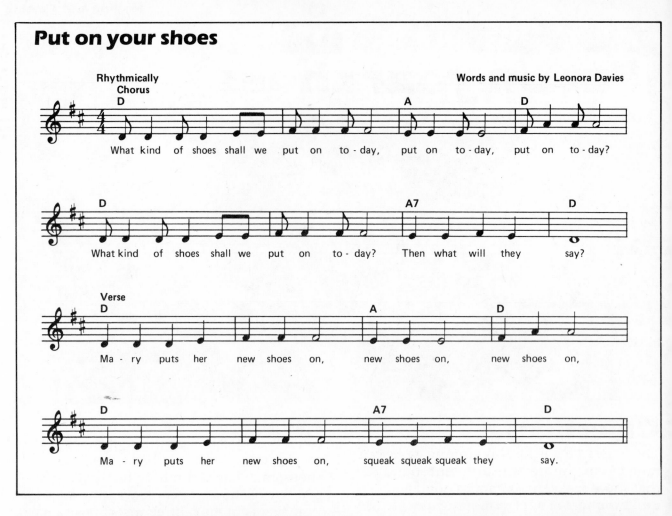

Rhythmically
Chorus

What kind of shoes shall we put on to-day, put on to-day, put on to-day?

What kind of shoes shall we put on to-day? Then what will they say?

Verse

Ma - ry puts her new shoes on, new shoes on, new shoes on,

Ma - ry puts her new shoes on, squeak squeak squeak they say.

You could pass a pair of shoes around the circle to decide who goes in the middle. Whoever is holding the shoes when the song stops is 'it'.

146

Bird in a cage

Objectives

This Japanese singing game allows for some individual singing and encourages the children to begin to discriminate aurally using each other's voices.

Level of development

Seven- to eight-year-olds.

Classroom organisation

Choose one person to sit in the centre and hide his eyes. The others all sit in a circle round him. As they sing the song the first time they pass a 'bird' gently round. At the end of the first time singing, one child will be left holding the bird. She goes into the middle and stands behind the child sitting there. The other children get up and as they

sing the song again walk slowly round. At 'Crane and tortoise . . .' they all sit down quietly and the child standing in the middle sings the last line 'Crane and tortoise all fall down, Who's behind you? Can you say?' The other child must try to guess who is singing. The game then proceeds with the child who was standing becoming the 'bird in the bamboo cage'.

Follow-up

Percussion instruments can be used to play this game with a smaller group of children. They sing the song in the same way with one child in the centre. Whoever is holding the bird after the first time of singing goes into the centre with their instrument. Instead of walking round all the other children sing and play quietly on the beat. On the last line they all stop as before. The child in the middle sings this line on his own and at the end plays the rhythm pattern of his name once or twice.

The song is also simple enough for beginner recorders to play. The last two bars only need three different notes: A, G and B. The game can be adapted so that instead of percussion instruments the children use their recorders. The game is played as before but with the last two bars played on the recorders rather than sung. The 'bird in the bamboo cage' must try to guess who it is as before.

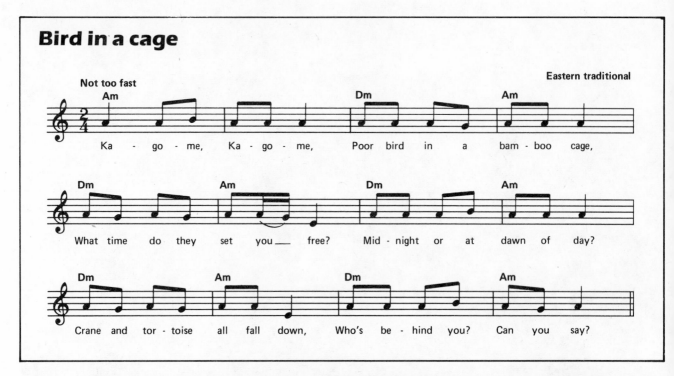

Bird in a cage

Not too fast

Eastern traditional

Ka - go - me, Ka - go - me, Poor bird in a bam - boo cage,

What time do they set you ___ free? Mid - night or at dawn of day?

Crane and tor - toise all fall down, Who's be - hind you? Can you say?

This song is simple enough to be played on a recorder.

Floating down the river

Objectives

This singing game underlines the musical ideas of contrasting speeds, fast and slow and demonstrates two different pulse beats.

Level of development

Six- to eight-year-olds.

Classroom organisation

Children join hands and circle round two children in the centre who keep the steady, gentle pulse beat with a 'rowing'

movement. At 'two in the middle' these children stand up and jump up and down to the different pulse beat whilst the others stand still and clap the beat. This section should be sung much louder and quicker. The two in the middle then choose partners and the song proceeds with the circle moving gently round and four rowers in the centre. These then increases to eight on the next verse. The final verse is 'Get out of there if you can't jump Josie . . . Oh my Susan Brown.'

All the children then join the circle and the game can proceed with a different pair of children in the centre. It might be more successful with younger children to build the game up with one child at a time and not have so many in the circle.

149

Floating down the river

American traditional

Fairly steady and smooth

We're float-ing down the riv-er, we're float-ing down be-low; We're

float-ing down the riv-er to the O-hi-o.

Fast

Two in the mid-dle and you can't jump Jo-sie, Two in the

mid-dle and you can't jump Jo-sie, Two in the mid-dle and you

can't jump Jo-sie, Oh, my Su-san Brown. _____
(Time to choose a friend.) _____

The children in the middle will need to dance to a different pulse beat.

Shay shay koolay

Objectives

This African song is an echo song providing the children with melodic patterns as well as rhythmic patterns. These can be used to great effect in the music area as the melody consists of only three notes: F, G and Bb. It can also be adapted as a circle singing game.

Level of development

Six- to eight-year-olds.

Classroom organisation

Arrange the children in two concentric circles so that each child has a partner. The inner circle sings the phrase and the outer one echoes. As they sing the children step round moving in opposite directions. On the last phrase they stop opposite a partner. They all clap the last phrase 'Kum a den day.' They sing the verse through a second time in the same way standing still, but this time they add a clapping pattern to each phrase which the partner must also echo back. The game can proceed round and next time each child should meet a different partner and try to invent different clapping patterns. This can also be extended to involve movement. As the children sing they make a movement which their partner must copy.

Follow-up

Working in pairs children can try out their clapping patterns on different instruments. One child plays a pattern on a tambourine which his partner must echo either on the same instrument or a different one.

151

Put out the three notes F, G and B♭ either on chime bars or select these notes on a xylophone or glockenspiel. Let the children work out the tune by ear. Working in pairs one child can play the melody whilst the other adds an accompaniment on an unpitched instrument – a drum/woodblock etc. This can either be the pulse beat or a rhythmic pattern (eg 'Langa chee langa') played over and over again. These in turn might be included in the singing game.

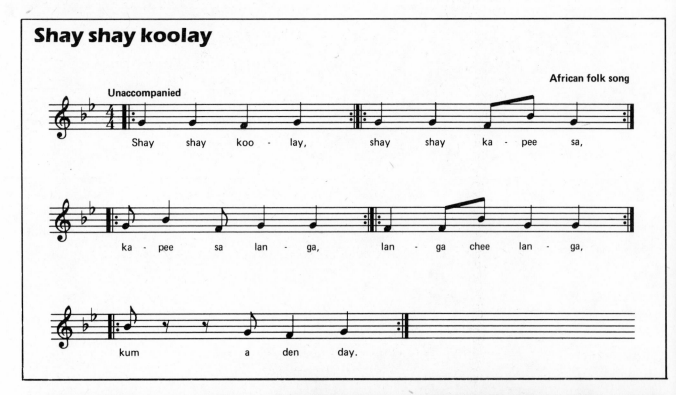

Shay shay koolay

African folk song

Unaccompanied

Shay   shay   koo - lay,   shay   shay   ka - pee   sa,

ka - pee   sa lan - ga,   lan - ga   chee   lan - ga,

kum   a   den   day.

Each time the circles stop each child will have a new partner.

152

The fireman's Hokey Cokey

Objectives

This is a simple circle dance based on the original Hokey Cokey (see page 83). As well as providing a bit of fun it might well link in with topic work for younger chilldren.

Level of development

Five- to six-year-olds.

Classroom organisation

Choose a child to go into the centre of the circle to lead the actions. Children who feel confident with the singing could even sing the first part of this song on their own. The rest of the class joins hands and dances round to the first part. When you get to 'you put your . . . ,' everyone stops and copies the child in the centre of the circle who goes through the appropriate actions. In the chorus everyone joins hands and dances into the centre and out again as in the original 'Hokey Cokey'. Repeat the chorus 'you put your . . .' a number of times getting faster each time.

Follow-up

It could be more fun if a 'set' of clothes were in the centre which the leader had to attempt to put on as she sings the words. Get different children to take the lead in the game.

The fireman's Hokey Cokey

Words and music by Leonora T. Davies

If you want to be a fire-man come ov-er here to me. You've

got to learn to dress so ve-ry rap-id-ly 'Cause when you

hear that bell man you've got to go _____ Can't hang back

Don't be slow You've got to learn the Fire-man's Ho-key Co-key,

You put your left leg in and the right one too

Pull on your trou-sers and you do the but-tons too, Next you take your jack-et put your

left and right sleeves in and do those but-tons right up to your chin.

Now what is there left to do? Pull on your big boots

one and two. Buck-le up your lea-ther belt there's one more thing to do,

Don't for-get your hel-met. Oh don't for-get your hel-met_____

oh don't for-get your hel-met_____ oh don't for-get your

hel-met_____ Now you've learned the fire-man's Ho-key Co-key.

Repeat ad lib. Each time faster

You put your left leg in and the right one too
Pull on your trousers and you do the buttons too.
Next you take your jacket, put your left and right
   sleeves in
And do those buttons right up to your chin.
Now what is there left to do?
Pull on your big boots one and two.

Buckle up your leather belt there's one more thing to
   do.
Don't forget your helmet . . . Oh don't forget your
   helmet
Oh don't forget your helmet. Oh don't forget your
   helmet
Now you've learned the fireman's Hokey Cokey.

Children enjoy this fun variation on the traditional Hokey Cokey.

155

Dancer in the ring

Objectives

This singing game is adapted freely and directly from the original singing game from Tobago 'Brown Gal in the Ring'. It offers young children an opportunity to dance imaginatively and freely within a corporate situation.

Level of development

Six- to eight-year-olds.

Classroom organisation

The children form a circle with someone in the centre. They step round, holding hands, and singing. On the last line of the first verse the children must sing about something that the 'dancer' is wearing. (You may like to decide this before starting the verse) 'and he's got a blue sweater on' . . . or 'and she's got a red skirt on'. In the second verse the 'dancer' must 'Show them the way to dance . . . .' All the children in the circle must copy what the dancer is doing.

The whole dance is repeated with a different 'dancer' in the centre. Try to encourage the children to be imaginative about the steps they use. You may like to discuss some ideas before they begin, eg step from side to side; point toes; pivot round; choose a partner etc.

156

Dancer in the ring

There's a dan - cer in the ring Tra - la - la - la la. There's a
Show us the way to dance.   Show us

dan - cer in the ring Tra - la - la - la There's a dan - cer in the ring
the way to dance.   Show us the way to dance.

Tra - la - la - la - la   And   he's   got   a   blue   sweat - er   on.
We   point   our   toes   like   this.
We   step   to   the   side   and   back.
We   all   chose   a   part - ner   and   skip.
We   twist   a - round   and   a -   round.

It helps to decide what item of clothing you are going to sing about first.

Ya tsa tsa via la la

Objectives

This is an Israeli singing game which has an interesting cumulative effect. It is useful when working with a large number of children as they all become involved very quickly.

Level of development

Six- to eleven-year-olds.

Classroom organisation

Children form a circle with one child in the centre. The children circle clockwise round singing 'La la'. The child in the centre walks in the opposite direction. On the word 'Eh' the child in the middle stands and faces whoever he is closest to. He beckons and moves into the centre of the circle. She follows him. Then she beckons and he follows her. On 'Clap and skip around . . .' the two join hands and dance around inside the circle together.

The game begins again with both children in the centre. The other children circle round them whilst they move in the opposite direction as before. The dance proceeds in the same way, only this time two children join those already in the centre. The next time there will be four and so on until everyone is dancing.

Ideally, of course, you need to have 32 etc participants but in practical terms this is probably unrealistic. The important thing is that everyone is participating. It is a useful activity for mixing up children who do not know each other well, as the choice of partners is quite arbitrary.

When children are not dancing they can clap on the pulse. This is always a useful activity as it helps to keep the beat and it emphasises the beat for the dancers.

Encourage children as far as possible to step and a dance *on* the beat. Children may like to find different ways of holding each other as they dance in pairs – ie holding hands; hands on shoulders; linking arms; arms around waist etc.

Y tsa tsa via la la

Jewish traditional

Quite fast

La la la la la la la
All circle and sing

la la la La la la la la EH ya tsa tsa vi-
Take a partner Beckon into the centre

a la la____ Ya tsa tsa vi-a la la____ Clap and skip a-
Partner beckons out again *Partners join hands and*

round and a-round and a-round and a-round and a-round and a-round.
dance around

The children might like to find different ways of dancing with their partners.

The big beast's boogie

Objectives

This dancing game will be a useful and appropriate link with project or topic work on dinosaurs. The movement and dance suggestions focus on contrasting sizes and shapes. The music uses a boogie style both in the rhythm and the melody and will require a reasonably competent pianist.

Level of development

Eight- to eleven-year-olds.

Classroom organisation

The song should be learned quite separately to the movement ideas. Although the words to the chorus are straightforward children will need to work hard on fitting the words and verses together. It is important not to sing it too quickly to begin with. Some suggestions for the dance have been given here. You may wish to adapt or modify them to suit your particular group of children or have your own ideas.

The big beasts

Organise the class into lines of four to six children. Each line should practise moving in unison as one monster. Try to work out a step pattern, in keeping with the rhythm of the song, that the children can do altogether. It might help if the children held onto each other's shoulders or waists. Encourage the leaders to make clear pathways and weave in and out of the other monster groups.

The spiky monsters

Working individually, encourage the children to grow slowly into spiky shapes, using elbows, hands and knees. Heads and feet can be used to make angular shapes. See if the children can jump suddenly to make another spiky shape.

Flying reptiles

Work on smooth, light, gliding movements with open, closing and turning actions. Encourage the children to use all of their bodies. Their wings should open and close from the centre of the body.

The water monsters

Work individually on sudden swooping actions, leading with the head. Try to add a running pattern to this swooping movement. Contrast this with slow rising, curving pathways. Try to get a 'break dance' kind of effect with a ripple movement running through the body.

The big beast's boogie

Did you hear about the party just the other night,
When the big beasts danced in the bright moonlight?
Well, they twisted and they boogied and they danced
    the whole night through,
Triceratops, Iguanodons and Brontosaurus too.

Chorus:
Come on and join the big beasts' party,
Come and hear the dinosaurus band.
There are carnivores and herbivores and lots of other
    great big jaws.
Dancing here upon the sand.

There was Stegosaurus jiving, oh beware his spikes,
But the Brontosaurus he just sat down.
Though they stayed there in the water where they
    swayed the whole night through,
Ichthyosaurus, Plesiosaurus joined the party too.

Chorus

The Pteranodons they glided up above their friends,
Every now and then they ate some fish.
Hypsilophodons, Iguanodons, their dancing was so
    neat,
Great big bodies, legs so short and tiny little feet.

Chorus

Though he did look rather savage with his three big
    horns,
Triceratops he waved his tail
When the king of all the dinosaurs,
    Tyrannosaurus Rex
Joined the party, goodness me, what's going to
    happen next!

Chorus

Costumes will help to make the song exciting.

The big beast's boogie

Boogie style
Not too fast

Words and music by Leonora Davies

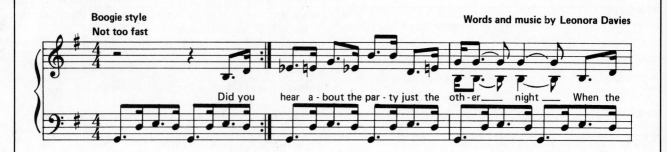

Did you hear a-bout the par-ty just the oth-er___ night ___ When the

big beasts_ danced ___ by the bright moon - light? Well, they twis-ted and they boog-ied and they

danced the whole night through Tri - ce - ra - tops, igu-an - o - dons and bron - to saur - us too

Chorus

come on___ and join the big beast par - ty ___ Come and hear the din - o-saur -us

There are car-ni-vores and her-bi-vores and lots of oth-er great big jaws

last time only

Dan-cing here up-on the sand. There was

English country garden

Objectives

This is a well-known melody taken from an original collection by Cecil Sharp. The steps have been adapted from a combination of English country dance ideas. Although the melody has four beats in a bar, the dance has a feel of 1 2 1 2.

163

Level of development

Six- to eight-year-olds.

Classroom organisation

It is advisable to teach this as a song before suggesting any dance steps. It may also be appropriate to divide the class into two groups and have one group singing whilst the other dances, as there are a number of words to remember. Alternatively you could tape record the children singing the song and play this for them to dance to. It is important to retain the gentleness of this song both for the singing and the movements.

For the first four bars the children move freely round the hall, stepping and counting 1 2 1 2 – as indicated on the music. They must then quickly find the nearest partner and link arms and step round in the same way (for four bars).

The steps for the following four bars are as follows:
First bar: Join hands and circle with small running steps.
Second bar: Running steps the other way.
Third bar: Stand facing partner. Point right toe forward and back then left toe forward and back.
Fourth bar: Link arms and circle round.

For the last four bars of the song the children break with their partners and dance individually.

The same actions are repeated for verses two and three, but this time children will find different partners.

Follow-up

This kind of dancing relies very much on counting. It will work well as a circle dance. The children circle to the right, holding hands, to a count of eight. They return in the same way to a count of eight. Let the children experiment to find the best kind of step for this purpose.

Let them work out suitable step for the next four bars with a partner. Try out various possibilities before deciding on one that everyone can do. Over the last four bars work out a way of changing partners. One possibility could be for the partners to start facing each other. They pass around the circle giving their right hands to their partner as they go then the left to the next partner counting eight until arriving at a new partner at the end of the song. Begin the next verse with the stepping to the right then back to the left but this time everyone should have a different partner to work with.

Using a tape of the song will make it easier for the children to learn the steps.

English country garden

How many gentle flowers grow
In an English country garden?
I'll tell you now of some I know
And those I miss I hope you'll pardon.
Daffodils, hearts-ease and phlox,
Meadow-sweet and lilies, stocks,
Gentle lupin and tall hollyhocks,
Roses, foxgloves, snowdrops, forget-me-nots
In an English country garden.

How many insects find their home
In an English country garden?
I'll tell you now of some I know
And those I miss I hope you'll pardon.
Dragonflies, moths and bees,
Spiders falling from the trees,
Butterflies sway in the mild, gentle breeze,
There are hedgehogs that roam and little gnomes
In an English country garden.

How many songbirds make their nests
In an English country garden?
I'll tell you now of some I know
And those I miss I hope you'll pardon.
Bab-bl-ing coo-cooing doves,
Robins and the warbling thrush,
Bluebird, lark, finch and nightingale
We all smile in the spring when the birds all start to
    sing
In an English country garden.

English country garden

How man-y gen-tle flow-ers___ grow in an Eng-lish coun-try
Step x   x   x   x   x   x

gar - den? I'll tell you now of some I___ know and those I
x   x   x   x   x   x

miss I hope you'll par - don. Daf - fo - dils, hearts-ease and phlox.
x   x   x   x

Mea - dow sweet and lil - ies, stocks Gen - tle lu - pin and

tall hol - ly hocks Rose fox - gloves, ___ snow - drops

for - get - me - nots in an Eng - lish coun - try gar - den.

On the first bar the children join hands with a partner and make small running steps.

Fred bear's ball

Objectives

A dancing game which combines a
corporate circle activity with an opportunity
for individual or partner dancing. Each
verse focuses on a particular way of
dancing: a march, a waltz, a tango and
skipping.

   The musical emphasis is on different
pulse groups/patterns. The combination of
singing and moving to different pulse
groups is an important development
process. Children need to feel and
experience pulse groups in a variety of ways
and all these ideas should be followed up
with instrumental and musical workshop
activities.

Level of development

Six- to nine-year-olds.

Classroom organisation

You may prefer to teach this as a song before
combining it with the dance suggestions.
Have the children make a circle and walk
round whilst they sing the chorus. Use the
first three notes with the pauses over them
to get ready. Encourage the children to step
together using two steps to each bar.

   During the verses drop hands but do
not move too far away from the circle

formation. It will take too long to re-form in time for the next chorus.

Verse 1 – children should march
Verse 2 – children should waltz
Verse 3 – children should tango. You may like to demonstrate the precise tango step if you know it or simply encourage children to feel the different rhythmic feature and make up their own dance step for it.
Verse 4 – children should skip

After each verse re-form the circle using the pause notes to make sure that everyone is ready.

Follow-up

The following activities can be used as part of an instrumental workshop. Each child will need an instrument. Let the children work in groups of three or four.

Activity 1

One child plays a pulse group using four beats on her drum

1234 1234 1234
>   >   >

The beat should be steady with an accent on the first beat. As she continues to play a second child joins in on a wood block. Then a third joins in on a triangle. A fourth child

could join in on a chime bar. They must listen to each other and keep together. Drop out in reverse order. Decide how long/how many times they will play the pattern. They could experiment playing loud and quiet.

Activity 2

Repeat Activity 1 using the same pulse group but choosing a different speed.

Activity 3

Repeat using a different pulse group (eg threes or fives).

Activity 4

One child plays a pulse group on her drum

123   123   123
>   >   >

She keeps this very steady and continues to play. A second child joins in with a rhythmic pattern using faster and slower notes. He continues and a third child joins in on a chime bar with a different pattern.

This is a more demanding activity and the children will need to have had other musical experiences. They will need to understand pulse groups so that they can come in with the rhythmic patterns on the first (accented) beat of the pulse group. It is, however, the kind of activity that they should be working towards. Class teachers may need to enlist the help of a music teacher for this activity.

Encourage the children to listen and dance to the different rhythms.

Fred bear's ball

Words and music by Leonora T. Davies

Chorus – not too fast but with a jaunty lilt

Oh would you like to come _____ to the Ted - dy Bears'

Ball. _____ It's just down there _____ a - long the

hall _____ Don't wor - ry a - bout your clothes _____

_ or your shoes or your bows _____ The bear in charge is

Fred the thread - bare bear as ev - ery - one knows.

Verse 1 – in march time, rhythmically

Now first we'll sim - ply march round in a line. Left, right, left, you're do - ing fine.

Turn to a part - ner Take their hand and keep on march - ing in time.

to chorus

Verse 2 – waltz time and lightly

Oh there is Jes - si - ca / Tim - o - thy Bear who is light on her / his toes,

she / he likes to waltz as eve - ry - one knows. One, two, three, one, it's as

sim - ple as that, come and join in the fun. _____ to chorus

Verse 3 – tango

You may be luck - y to see a won - der - ful sight, Sa - hid and Sue all

dressed in white Dance their Tan - go toss - ing their heads, Let us join in with them.

to chorus

Verse 4 – skip, fast

And last of all a step that eve - ry - one knows, skip and clap and

round you go smil - ing as you turn and spin, Eve - ry - one join in.

to chorus

Dipidu

Objectives

This folk song from Uganda illustrates a change from a three-beat pulse pattern to a two-beat pulse pattern. The addition of simple movements helps to reinforce this musical idea.

Level of development

Six- to eight-year-olds.

Classroom organisation

For Part 1 (three beats) the children walk around freely, singing the verse and smiling at friends as they go. For Part 2 (two beats) they must stand still and face the first partner that they come to and clap hands together. It will be useful if each child has made up a pattern to clap before they come to sing the song through. When the song is repeated the children will meet a different partner for Part 2.

Follow-up

An addition to the song could be that each part is accompanied by a different instrument keeping the steady pulse count of two or three. It could be a wood block for three beats and a drum for two beats. Make sure the children playing the instruments accent the first beat in each pattern.

Dipidu

At a walking pace

Ugandan folk song

Good - day, good - day to you, Good - day, O dip - i - du,

Dip, dip, dip - i - du, Dip - i - du, O dip - i - du.

Dip, dip, dip, dip, dip - i - du, Dip - i - du, O dip - i - du.

Bow bow oh Belinda

Objectives

This is a more formal traditional American country dance. The children will need to be able to co-ordinate skipping movements and to count carefully as they listen to the musical phrases.

171

Level of development

Eight- to eleven-year-olds.

Classroom organisation

Learn the simple melody before adding any dance steps. It is always helpful to encourage the children to feel the first beat of each bar by clapping or swaying as they sing. In this particular dancing game when the children have done this, get them to feel each beat, ie two counts to each bar. This will help when they come to count and dance the steps.

It is not necessary to pair the children off in girl/boy partners for this dance. However, for the purpose of explaining the dance steps that formation has been used here. The children form two equal lines, one of girls and one of boys (five to seven couples in all).

The top boy and bottom girl meet, stepping 1 2 3, then nod and back 2 3 4 (eight counts altogether).

The top girl meets the bottom boy in exactly the same way 1 2 3, nod, back 2 3 4 (eight counts).

The partners face each other and swing round together to the right for eight counts, then back to the left for eight counts.

The top couple then joins hands and side steps down the centre of the lines whilst the others clap as they go (eight counts).

Everyone joins hands with their partner and swings round for another eight counts. The children will have sung all three verses. They can be repeated as often as necessary until all the couples have had a turn at the top.

Follow-up

Repeat the first part of the dance as previously described, ie eight counts followed by eight counts.

You can vary the way the partners dance together. They can link arms and dance round to the right then the left; hold boths hands; do a 'Do-si-do' behind their backs or in front of them at shoulder level and skip out to meet their partner, skip round each other back to back and back to their places.

A variant to the last eight counts is for the top couple to lead their lines to the outside, turning away from their partner. All the others follow on each line. The top couple meets at the bottom and forms an arch. The others find their partners as they come to the arch and dance through it. This formation will ensure that a new couple is now at the top of the formation.

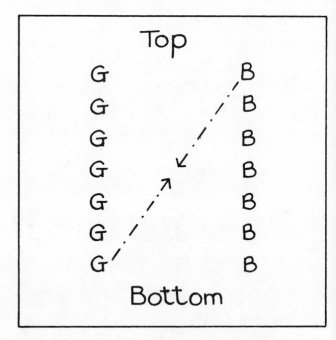

Change the words of the verses to describe the movements, ie 'Both hands round Belinda' or 'Do-si-do around Belinda' or 'Follow my leader round Belinda'.

Verse 1
Bow bow oh Belinda × 3
Won't you be my partner?
Verse 2
Right hand around Belinda × 2
Left hand around Belinda
Won't you be my partner?
Verse 3
Down the middle Oh Belinda × 2
Swing your partner round and round
Won't you be my partner?

A very simple two note accompaniment can be played on any pitched instrument. Try adding a drum or a tambourine to keep the steady pulse beat.

172

Bow bow oh Belinda

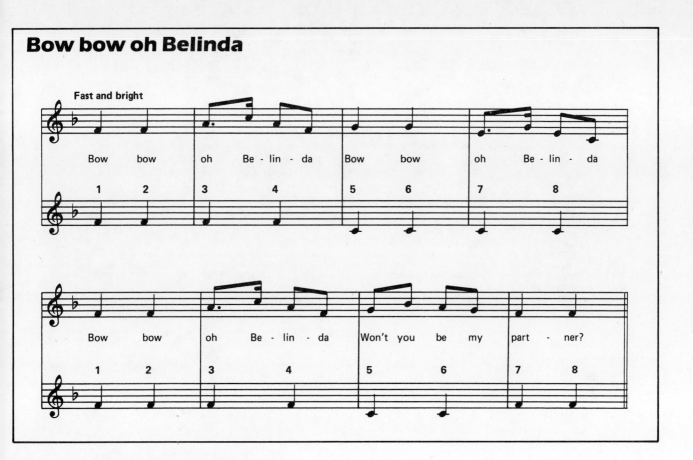

Resources

Sound Waves Leonora Davies, Bell & Hyman
(1986)

Season of mists and
mellow fruitfulness.
John Keats
Oak
Apples
Bread

Poems

Poems

INTRODUCTION

Leonora Davies has had many years of teaching experience at all levels of education from infants to higher education. She is presently music co-ordinator with the ILEA; working alongside teachers in the classroom, setting up in-service activities and generally co-ordinating music-making events. Her publications include *Sound Waves* published by Bell & Hyman and the *Primary Music Course* published by Oxford University Press. She is a frequent contributor of both articles and songs to *Child* and *Junior Education* and has also produced and compiled many resource cassettes for Scholastic Publications.

The first poems children hear, whatever their culture or primary language, are their nursery rhymes, action rhymes, finger play games and playground chants. In general these appeal because of the rhythmic, repetitious, 'musical' use of language. They may also appeal in part because of the nonsensical ideas presented in them, or they may appeal because of the strangely imaginative elements embodied in many of them. Whatever the precise appeal, young children love to find their favourite rhymes in books and delight in hearing them read aloud, over and over again. Some of these favourites 'old and new' can be found elsewhere in this book. They provide us with an important basis upon which we can encourage children to begin to develop an understanding of language. They provide children with important clues for helping them to understand their culture. However as children grow in awareness and begin to explore the environment, beyond the home and the nursery school, they need to be presented with a wide variety of opportunities to explore language and a variety of linguistic structures. Once children have a sufficient understanding of language for them to enjoy poetry and verse for its content as well as its pleasurable sound, they must be offered more than the much-loved nursery rhymes.

Poetry is a very personal form of expression. The very nature of a poem or a verse may be defined by adults in a variety of different ways. For some, poems need to rhyme, others may accept poetry as lines which scan. Others may just appreciate the precise and selective use of language. Others may describe it as the manipulating and juxtaposing of words to mean more than they say at first glance.

It is this personal ingredient of poetry that makes teaching it so difficult, yet it is one of the most important reasons why this form of expression should be presented and made widely accessible to children.

This chapter seeks to address some of these issues and answer some of the questions that teachers might raise when choosing, preparing, presenting and sharing poetry, verses and poetic ideas with children.

How to select appropriate material

In choosing verse, as with choosing stories, teachers must be guided by their knowledge of the needs of their children – their need to assimilate experiences, their need to be understood, their need to clarify their knowledge and their need to explore.

Type of material to choose

Children need to be presented with a wide variety of material ranging from traditional verse, narrative poems, poems about familiar things, amusing and nonsensical poems and poems that involve the imagination and sense of wonder. Examples of these categories can be found in this chapter. The Resources list (see page 194) contains anthologies where you will find many more poems from each of the above categories.

How can you use poetry in the classroom? What else can you do with poems apart from read them? Where shall you find appropriate material? This chapter contains ideas and suggestions which may answer some of these important questions. It is impossible to be definitive or categoric in making these suggestions. All the ideas will need to be developed to suit your particular and individual group of children. If you want a really comprehensive anthology for use with your own group of children then you must compile one of your own, taking care to include poems to suit every occasion, every interest and every mood.

Children can help to compile a classroom anthology of their favourite poems.

Types of poetry

Traditional verses

Derby ram

As I was going to Derby, Sir, 'twas on a summer's
day,
I met the finest ram, Sir, that ever was fed on hay,
And indeed, Sir, 'tis true, Sir, I never was given to lie,
And if you'd been to Derby, Sir, you'd have seen him as
well as I.

It had four feet to walk on, Sir, it had four feet to
stand,
And every foot it had, Sir, did cover an acre of land.

And indeed, Sir, 'tis true, Sir, I never was given to lie,
And if you'd been to Derby, Sir, you'd have seen him as
well as I.

This ram it had a horn, Sir, that reached up to the
sky,
The birds went up and built their nests, could hear
the young ones cry.
And indeed, Sir, 'tis true, Sir, I never was given to lie,
And if you'd been to Derby, Sir, you'd have seen him as
well as I.

This ram he had another horn that reached up to the
   moon,
The birds went up in January and didn't come down
   till June.
And indeed, Sir, 'tis true, Sir, I never was given to lie,
And if you'd been to Derby, Sir, you'd have seen him as
   well as I.

And all the men of Derby, Sir, came begging for his
   tail,
To ring St George's passing-bell at the top of Derby
   jail.
And indeed, Sir, 'tis true, Sir, I never was given to lie,
And if you'd been to Derby, Sir, you'd have seen him as
   well as I.

And all the women of Derby, Sir, came begging for
   his ears,
To make them leather aprons to last them forty years.
And indeed, Sir, 'tis true, Sir, I never was given to lie,
And if you'd been to Derby, Sir, you'd have seen him as
   well as I.

And all the boys of Derby, Sir, came begging for his
   eyes,
To make a pair of footballs, for they were just the
   size.
And indeed, Sir, 'tis true, Sir, I never was given to lie,
And if you'd been to Derby, Sir, you'd have seen him as
   well as I.

The butcher that killed this ram, Sir, was in danger of
   his life,
He was up to his knees in blood crying out for a
   longer knife.
And indeed, Sir, 'tis true, Sir, I never was given to lie,
And if you'd been to Derby, Sir, you'd have seen him as
   well as I.

And now my song is ended, I have no more to say,
So please will you give us a New Year's gift, and let
   us go away.
And indeed, Sir, 'tis true, Sir, I never was given to lie,
And if you'd been to Derby, Sir, you'd have seen him as
   well as I.

Who killed Cock Robin?

Who killed Cock Robin?
   I, said the Sparrow,
   With my bow and arrow,
I killed Cock Robin.

Who saw him die?
   I, said the Fly,
   With my little eye,
I saw him die.

Who caught his blood?
   I, said the Fish,
   With my little dish,
I caught his blood.

Who'll make his shroud?
   I, said the Beetle,
   With my thread and needle,
I'll make his shroud.

Who'll dig his grave?
   I, said the Owl,
   With my spade and trowel,
I'll dig his grave.

Who'll carry the link?
   I, said the Linnet,
   I'll come in a minute,
I'll bear the link.

Who'll be the parson?
   I, said the Rook,
   With my little book,
I'll be the parson.

Who'll carry him to his grave?
   I, said the Kite,
   If it's not in the night,
I'll carry him to the grave.

Who'll be chief mourner?
   I, said the Dove,
   I mourn for my love.
I'll be chief mourner.

Who'll bear the pall?
   We, said the Wren,
   Both the cock and the hen,
We'll bear the pall.

Who'll sing a psalm?
   I, said the Thrush,
   As she sat in a bush,
I'll sing a psalm.

Who'll toll the bell?
   I, said the Bull,
   Because I can pull,
I'll toll the bell.

   And so Robin, Farewell!

And all the birds of the air
Fell a-sighing and a-sobbing,
When they heard of the death
   Of poor Cock Robin.

Anonymous

A lyke-wake dirge

This ae night, this ae night,
Every night and all;
Fire and sleete and candle light,
And Christ receive thy saul.

When thou from hence away art past,
Every night and all;
To Whinny-muir thou comest at last;
And Christ receive thy saul.

If ever thou gavest hosen and shoon,
Every night and all;
Sit thee down and put them on;
And Christ receive thy saul.

If hosen and shoon thou ne'er gavest nane,
Every night and all;
The whinnes shall prick thee to the bare bane
And Christ receive thy saul.

From Whinny-muir when thou mayest pass,
Every night and all;
To Brigg o'Dread thou comest at last;
Then Christ receive they saul.

From Brigg o'Dread when thou mayest pass,
Every night and all;
To purgatory fire thou comest at last;
And Christ receive thy saul.

If ever thou gavest meat or drink,
Every night and all;
The fire shall never make thee shrink;
And Christ receive thy saul.

If meat or drink thou never gavest nane,
Every night and all;
The fire will burn thee to the bare bane;
And Christ receive thy saul.

This ae night, this ae night,
Every night and all;
Fire and sleete and candle light;
And Christ receive thy saul.

Anonymous

Meet-on-the-Road

'Now, pray, where are you going?' said Meet-on-the-Road.
'To school, sir, to school, sir,' said Child-as-it-Stood.

'What have you in your basket, child?' said Meet-on-the-Road.
'My dinner, sir, my dinner, sir,' said Child-as-it-Stood.

'What have you for dinner, child?' said Meet-on-the-Road.
'Some pudding, sir, some pudding, sir,' said Child-as-it-Stood.

'Oh, then I pray, give me a share,' said Meet-on-the-Road.
'I've little enough for myself, sir,' said Child-as-it-Stood.

'What have you got that cloak on for?' said Meet-on-the-Road.
'To keep the wind and cold from me,' said Child-as-it-Stood.

'I wish the wind would blow through you,' said Meet-on-the-Road.
'Oh, what a wish! What a wish!' said Child-as-it-Stood.

'Pray what are those bells ringing for?' said Meet-on-the-Road.
'To ring bad spirits home again,' said Child-as-it-Stood.

'Oh, then I must be going, child!' said Meet-on-the-Road.
'So fare you well, so fare you well,' said Child-as-it-Stood.

Anonymous

Narrative verse

Night mail

This is the night mail crossing the border,
Bringing the cheque and the postal order,
Letters for the rich, letters for the poor,
The shop at the corner and the girl next door.
Pulling up Beattock, a steady climb –
The gradient's against her, but she's on time.

Past cotton grass and moorland boulder,
Shovelling white steam over her shoulder,
Snorting noisily as she passes
Silent miles of wind-bent grasses.

Birds turn their heads as she approaches,
Stare from the bushes at her black-faced coaches.
Sheep-dogs cannot turn her course,
They slumber on with paws across.
In the farm she passes no one wakes,
But a jug in the bedroom gently shakes.

Dawn freshens, the climb is done.
Down towards Glasgow she descends
Towards the steam tugs yelping down the glade of
    cranes,
Towards the fields of apparatus, the furnaces
Set on the dark plain like gigantic chessmen.
All Scotland waits for her:
In the dark glens, beside the pale-green lochs
Men long for news.

Letters of thanks, letters from banks,
Letters of joy from girl and boy,
Receipted bills and invitations
To inspect new stock or visit relations,
And applications for situations
And timid lovers' declarations
And gossip, gossip from all the nations.

News circumstantial, news financial,
Letters with holiday snaps to enlarge in,
Letters with faces scrawled in the margin,
Letters from uncles, cousins, and aunts,
Letters to Scotland from the South of France,
Letters of condolence to Highlands and Lowlands,
Notes from overseas to Hebrides –

Written on paper of every hue,
The pink, the violet, the white and the blue,
The chatty, the catty, the boring, adoring,
The cold and official and the heart outpouring,
Clever, stupid, short and long,
The typed and printed and the spelt all wrong.

Thousands are still asleep
Dreaming of terrifying monsters,
Or of friendly tea beside the band at Cranston's or
    Crawford's,
Asleep in working Glasgow, asleep in well-set
    Edinburgh,
Asleep in granite Aberdeen,
They continue their dreams;
And shall wake soon and long for letters,
And none will hear the postman's knock
Without a quickening of the heart,
For who can hear and feel himself forgotten?

W H Auden

The song the train sang

Now
When
Steam hisses;
Now
When the
Coupling clashes;
Now
When the
Wind rushes
Come the slow but sudden swaying,
Every truck and carriage trying
For a smooth and better rhythm.

This . . . is . . . the . . . one . . .
That . . . is . . . the . . . one . . .
This is the one,
That is the one,
This is the one, that is the one,
This is the one, that is the one . . .

Over the river, past the mill,
Through the tunnel under the hill;
Round the corner, past the wall,
Through the wood where trees grow tall.
Then in sight of the town by the river,
Brake by the crossing where white leaves quiver.
Slow as the streets of the town slide past
And the windows stare
                at the jerking of the coaches
Coming into the station approaches.

Stop at the front.
Stop at the front.
Stop . . . at the front.
Stop . . . at the . . .
Stop.

AHHHHH!

Neil Adams

Legend

The blacksmith's boy went out with a rifle
And a black dog running behind.
Cobwebs snatched at his feet,
Rivers hindered him,
Thorn-branches caught at his eyes to make him blind
And the sky turned into an unlucky opal,
But he didn't mind.
*I can break branches, I can swim rivers, I can stare out
    any spider I meet,*
Said he to his dog and his rifle.

The blacksmith's boy went over the paddocks
With his old black hat on his head.
Mountains jumped in his way,
Rocks rolled down on him,
And the old crow cried, *You'll soon be dead;*
And the rain came down like mattocks.
But he only said
*I can climb mountains, I can dodge rocks, I can shoot an
    old crow any day.*
And he went on over the paddocks.

When he came to the end of the day the sun began
    falling.
Up came the night ready to swallow him,
Like the barrel of a gun,
Like an old black hat,
Like a black dog hungry to follow him.
Then the pigeon, the magpie and the dove began
    wailing,
And the grass lay down to pillow him.
His rifle broke, his hat blew away and his dog was
    gone,
And the sun was falling.

But in front of the night the rainbow stood out on the
    mountain
Just as his heart foretold.
He ran like a hare,
He climbed like a fox,
He caught it in his hands, the colours and the cold –
Like a bar of ice, like the columns of a fountain,
Like a ring of gold.
The pigeon, the magpie and the dove flew up to
    stare,
And the grass stood up again on the mountain.

The blacksmith's boy hung the rainbow on his
    shoulder,
Instead of his broken gun.
Lizards ran out to see,
Snakes made way for him,
And the rainbow shone as brightly as the sun.
All the world said, *Nobody is braver, nobody is bolder,
Nobody else has done
Anything to equal it.* He went home as easy as could
    be
With the swinging rainbow on his shoulder.

Judith Wright

Amusing poems

Mice

I think mice
Are rather nice.

Their tails are long,
Their faces small,
They haven't any
Chins at all.
Their ears are pink,
Their teeth are white,
They run about
The house at night.
They nibble things
They shouldn't touch
And no one seems
To like them much.

But I think mice
Are nice.

Rose Fyleman

A baby sardine

A baby sardine
saw her first submarine;
she was scared and watched through
a peephole.

'Oh come, come, come,'
said the sardine's mum,
'It's only a tin full of people.'

Spike Milligan

Poems about familiar things

In the sun

Sit
on your doorstep
or any place.

Sit
in the sun
and lift your face.

Close your eyes and
sun dream.
Soon the warm sun
will seem
to fill you up
and
spill over.

Lilian Moore

August afternoon

Where shall we go?
    What shall we play?
What shall we do
    On a hot summer day?

We'll sit in the swing.
    Go low. Go high.
And drink lemonade
    Till the glass is dry.

One straw for you,
    One straw for me,
In the cool green shade
    Of the walnut tree.

Marion Edey

There's a red brick wall

There's a red brick wall
    along our street
that stands and burns
    in the sun's hot heat.

There aren't any flames
    but I know it burns.
When I walk by,
    it glows and turns
    my face to fire.

Nancy Chambers

Poems that involve a sense of wonder

Who's that?

Who's that
stopping at
my door in the
dark, deep
in the dead of the moonless night?

Who's
that in the quiet
blackness,
darker than dark?

Who turns the han-
dle of my door, who
turns the old brass hand-
le of
my door with never a sound, the handle
that always
creaks and rattles and
squeaks but
now
turns
without a sound, slowly
slowly
    slowly
        round?

Who's that moving through the floor
as if it were a lake, an open door? Who
is it who passes through
what can never be passed though,

who passes through
the rocking-chair
without rocking it,
who passes through
the table without knocking it, who
walks out of the cupboard without unlocking it?
Who's that? Who plays with my toys
with no noise, no
noise?

Who's that? Who is it
silent and silver
as things in mirrors, who's
as slow as feathers,
shy as the shivers,
light as a fly?

Who's that who's that
as close as
close as a hug, a kiss –
Who's THIS?

James Kirkup

Snow

White bird featherless
Flew from paradise,
Perched on the castle wall;
Along came Lord Landless
Took it up handless
And rode away horseless to the King's white hall.

Anon

183

The snowman's song

I fell down from the sky
   One moony night
   In feathery flakes
   Of sparkling white,
And settled where I fell
   Without a sound
   On the bare trees
   And the dark ground.

Then shouting children came
   Excitedly
   They scooped me up
   And moulded me
Into this comfy shape
   The snowman tall
   Who stands beside
   The garden wall.

And every day the sun
   Shines down on me,
   Makes me as bright
   As bright can be.
I stand here now and watch
   You as you play
   Then one hot day
   I'll melt away.

I'll simply melt away
   One hot, hot day . . .
     Away, away,
     Away

Poems as a stimulus for writing

Objectives

A great deal of writing work can be developed from talking about poems. This could take the form of direct discussion about a specific poem that has been read aloud to the class, where children share and pool ideas to develop a corporate understanding of the poem. In this way children will begin to extend their vocabulary, to acquire an insight into someone else's imagination and to understand some of the skills and techniques of manipulating words and phrases. This organisational and compositional craft is essential if children are going to develop their writing skills. This process cannot be rushed, however, and must be built on gradually. It is essential, to begin with, that children are stimulated and encouraged to express themselves freely.

Level of development

Seven- to eleven-year-olds.

Classroom organisation

Class discussion in general can often be a source of stimulus for writing. However, the teacher can and should guide and direct discussion so as to focus on 'skills' which contribute both directly and indirectly to developing children's writing abilities, in particular to their poetic writing skills.

Through discussion teachers can encourage children to develop a greater awareness – to help them develop a 'seeing eye'. There are a number of activities that can help to foster this kind of awareness.

Ask another teacher/pupil to pay a fleeting visit to the class. Then ask the children to describe, in as much detail as they can, the appearance of this person. This can be done as a 'writing' or 'conversation' exercise or it can be done with children working in pairs. Ask them to try to remember together as much as they can. Working in pairs allows children to progress more easily at their 'own' pace and is a useful way of encouraging more inhibited pupils to participate. Later ask the 'visitor' to come back so that children can check the accuracy of their descriptions.

Another possibility might be for the children to each prepare an anonymous 'pen portrait' of a friend, with plenty of interesting detail but no name mentioned. Other children can then try to guess 'Who's who?' Once the children have worked on this idea using prose, encourage them to refine their writing to choose the most important details thus working it into a more 'poetic' structure.

Writing riddles can be useful and great fun. It will encourage children to look closely at the chosen subject and to make a careful search for words to describe it. The idea is to give clues which are interesting and accurate without actually naming the object. See children's examples on page 187.

The poem 'Golden boy' by Ted Hughes or Kevin Crossley Holland's translations of Anglo-Saxon riddles will provide useful models for children to examine. They may enjoy producing their own contemporary versions.

One of the essences of effective writing is precision. By extending children's experiences you will be helping them to be specific and to avoid generalisation. Wallace Steven's poem, 'Thirteen ways of looking at a blackbird', which can be found in a number of anthologies may be rather taxing for primary children, but his idea can be borrowed to encourage them to look beyond the first automatic response. Children need to be encouraged to think of all five senses, and not just sight. Games such as the following simple word association can be useful preparations for writing.

Word associations can be played with a clapping pattern.

Word associations

Have one child set up a clapping pattern with a steady and regular beat. The pattern should be made up of claps and gaps. The length of the gap should be equivalent to an equal number of claps.
2 XX– –XX– –XX– –XX– – or
3 XXX– – –XXX– – –XXX– – – or
4 XXXX– – – –XXXX– – – –XXXX– – – – and
   so on.
Make the gaps with an 'open hand' gesture.

To begin with, take all these patterns at a fairly leisurely pace. When everyone has joined in with the clapping pattern, the first child thinks of a word and says it in the gap. Proceeding round the circle, the next child must say a word into the next gap which has some association with the first word. The activity continues in this way. To begin with, if someone misses the gap or is unable to think quickly enough, let them find the next appropriate gap. It is important for everyone to keep the clapping pattern going. Later you can devise some kind of 'forfeit' for people who miss.

Extend this idea into a preparatory exercise for writing. Let each child write the starting point in the centre on a piece of paper. Leave the children to write down absolutely anything which comes to mind when he hears the chosen word. Always encourage children to use as many senses as possible. It is ironically easy for children to lose early on, the capacity for experiencing relatively simple things at anything more than a very superficial level. Careful encouragement in different ways of seeing is one way in which we can work in the classroom to deepen those experiences through discussion and writing.

One particular 'style' of poetry writing which can serve as a very useful model for children is that of Japanese Haiku. Children sometimes get bogged down and confused when attempting to write long poems, particularly if they try to force a rhyme on a poem too.

Haiku are short epigrammatic Japanese poems consisting of 17 syllables altogether. They are generally arranged as a line of five, a line of seven and a line of five and they do not usually rhyme.

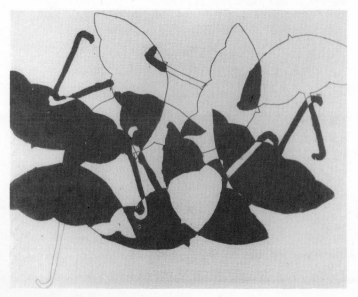

Sudden shower

Not even a hat –	5 syllables
and cold rain falling on me?	7 syllables
Tut-tut. Think of that.	5 syllables

Matzuo Basho Translated by H G Henderson

Spring rain

Scampering over saucers –
The sound of a rat.
Cold, cold.

Spring rain:
Telling a tale as they go,
Straw cape, umbrella.

Sudden shower:
Grasping the grass-blades
A shoal of sparrows.

Spring rain:
A man lives here –
Smoke through the wall.

Mosquito-buzz
Whenever honeysuckle
Petals fall.

Spring rain:
Soaking on the roof
A child's rag ball.

Yosa Buson Translated by Bownas and Thwaite

Haiku encourage children to be precise and selective in their use and choice of words and phrases. With a little practice children can create striking and effective images. The following two examples of Haiku were written by children after class discussion on 'How many different things can you tell me that are to do with night and night time?' The discussion eventually focused on the moon. The teacher encouraged the children to think beyond the superficial and look towards a deeper and less clichéd view of the subject.

The moon's a great ball
Like a hole in the darkness
With clouds around it.
(*Boy aged 11*)

A big white light bulb
With no electricity
In a big black lamp.
(*Girl aged 11*)

The following three Haiku have been written on the well-worn theme of Christmas by ten-year-old children.

Presents big and small
Wrapping paper everywhere
Children love it all.

Falling on the ground
Snowflakes make no sound at all
Silence all around.

Shepherds and wise men
They all came to see Jesus
Lying in his bed.

Although the framework of five, seven, five syllables has been given it is not completely necessary to keep to this. Many of the Japanese Haiku have different syllable patterns though they probably conform in the original Japanese.

All the following poems are examples of children's writing. Many of the examples are the result of work produced after the initial stimulus of class discussion and some of the 'exercises' suggested.

The dream

Out of the blackness of the night
Came a yell, a scream, a dream and a shout.
Together they hovered over the hill,
Together they hovered to a window sill.

They crept through a crack in the window frame
And then they ran into a brain
Of a girl who was lying still again.

Screams, shouts, yells and shrieks
Were heard inside her head.
This terrible noise went on and on
All through the night in bed.
(*Girl aged 11*)

The press

The everlasting chattering of machines
Goes on through the night
Turning out all the information
Fed into their one-night minds.
War, peace, robbery, scandal, entertainment,
Anything else a money-searching person can find.
The comments of unheard people,
No one will ever see their views of the matter,
Printed in black and white.
(*Girl aged 11*)

A scream of fear
Exposes me to night.
A gradual descent
Admits the wind.
Fear of night
Holds me
Imprisoned in my room,
Encased by a bar of moonlight
Nailed to my door
While slates rush down past me
Knocking at my window.
(*Girl aged 11*)

I stand before night
And its terrors,
Its only conqueror is light.
It is like a letter bomb addressed to earth,
Like God putting a black sheet over us
To keep us quiet.
(*Boy aged 11*)

Snow

I am white
And I fall from a hedge
I cover the ground
And I don't make a sound.
(*Boy aged 8*)

Pearls on the grass

After the beautiful rain
The rocks shine under the sun
Like the droplets on the cobweb
Amongst the green, green grass.
(*Geeta Monhanty aged 13*)

Two riddles

It's two weeks old.
It does what it's told.
It can't talk and it can't walk.
It is very brainy,
very, very brainy.
(*Andrew – 'Our Computer'*)

I live in the summer
in the merry month of May.
I taste bitter and sour,
my milky insides taste the same.
I often grow in fields
and I am yellow and green.
What am I?
(*Elizabeth – 'Dandelion'*)

187

Reflections

On the moors it is very quiet
On your own.
There's nobody around
Except yourself.
It's peaceful there
When you stop and think.
Stone walls at the back of you
Maybe a few donkeys on the moor.
There's no more noise of the war
For you to listen for.
No more screaming, no more shouting
Just peace and quiet.
No more Hasting of the bombs
Just green grass for miles and miles
All is dead
Except yourself
You're on the moors alone
No friend with you!
This is real peace.
(*Wendy Maggs aged 11*)

He is a sad dragon waiting his chance;
He waits for the world to change again.
His ancestors were the kings of the earth
And he watches with his beady eye
For something to fall out of the sky
So that he can roam about free
Like dinosaurs from out of the sea.
(*Mark aged 11*)

Poems as a stimulus for music making

Objectives

To use poems as a stimulus for a variety of musical work.

Level of development

Five- to eleven-year-olds.

Classroom organisation

The suggestions that are developed here involve children working on their own in music areas. It is important for children to be given opportunities to develop musical ideas in their own time, working individually, in pairs or in small groups. Let them make their own decisions, explore and experiment with sounds and develop new or existing skills.

This pre-supposes that a table or a special area of the classroom can be set aside for children to work in this way (see page 118). It may mean that it is only used at specific times of the day. This is quite understandable in a busy primary classroom.

It is also vital that the children's work is properly acknowledged – time to listen to children's pieces will need to be set aside. It is also important that the children are stimulated to work in the music area with some kind of a structured activity. This may take the form of a photograph, a poem, a story, a three-dimensional object or particular instruments that have been selected for the week/day.

One of the 'dangers' of putting music and organised sounds with poems or stories is that children often simply produce a series of sound effects which have little musical quality. Teachers must help and encourage the children to think beyond this superficial stage, in the same way that was suggested in the section on Poems as a stimulus for writing.

Developing common elements between subject areas can help children to think more deeply and to organise their ideas more clearly. To give an example, think of three particular elements – contrasts, changes and comparisons. These might be developed in terms of colour, form, language and movement. They are also important elements of music:

Loud/quiet   contrasts
Getting louder/quieter   changes
Louder than/quieter than   comparisons

Poetry can provide a parallel which encourages the children to think, explore and experiment in a more probing way. Begin with two poems with completely contrasting moods.

A variety of instruments and sound sources should be made available. It is often useful to begin this kind of work – as with the writing stimulus – with a class discussion. Read the poems aloud and let the children enjoy and become familiar with the language and the content. Display the poems in the music area or copy them onto individual cards so that the children have proper access to them.

Fog

Soft fog falls,
Silent on the town,
It encloses everyone,
On his small island,
All alone,
Then drifts off.

                                   Anonymous

The railway station

Trains coming in,
Trains going out,
Buzzing, screeching,
Grinding, scraping.

Whizzing past you,
Not caring for you,
Whistles whistling,
Brakes screeching.

People running,
People walking,
Shuffling, scuffling,
Along the wide crowded platform.

People get on the trains,
Opening and shutting doors,
The platform is almost deserted,
People no longer exist there.
(*Gwyneth aged 11*)

The class discussion needs to ensure that the children understand the vocabulary, the ideas and the images. How does the poet capture the atmosphere in each poem? How might that be expressed in musical ideas? It is important that children share some of their ideas so that everyone has some kind of initial starting idea for their music. Contrast, for instance, the rhythmic qualities of 'The railway station'

189

Children need to have time to develop their ideas on their own in the music area.

with the timeless atmosphere created in 'Fog'.

It may be that children will recite the poems and work their musical ideas into this. They may choose to work on the contrasting atmospheres created by the words and try to develop the same mood in their music. Or they could just select some of the effective 'sound words' from each poem and use these as a vocal accompaniment to the spoken poems. This would mean that children were just working with their voices. They might develop these 'sound words' quite independently of the poems – words such as 'silent', 'drifts', 'soft'. They may prefer to abandon the poems as such altogether and develop the ideas of dynamic (loud/quiet) contrasts. The poems will still have been a valuable initial stimulus.

Encouraging the children to group and select instruments with contrasting timbres (sound qualities) is another way of helping them to structure and organise their musical ideas. Two contrasting groups of instruments could provide very satisfactory

musical involvement for the following two poems. The basic stimulus is still rooted in the idea of contrasts.

And it was windy weather

Now the winds are riding by;
Clouds are galloping the sky;

Bush and tree are lashing bare,
Savage boughs on savage air;

Crying, as they lash and sway,
Pull the roots out of the clay.

Lift away; away;
Away.

Leave security, and speed
From the root, the mud and mead.

Into sea and air, we go.
To chase the gull, the moon – and know

Flying high
Flying high.

All the freedom of the sky
All the freedom of the sky.

James Stephens

The tide in the river

The tide in the river,
The tide in the river,
The tide in the river runs deep.

I saw a shiver
pass over the river
As the tide turned in its sleep.   Eleanor Farjeon

Begin this work in the same way as suggested before, with a class discussion. Although the children, after the initial corporate preparation, will be working either individually, in small groups or in pairs it is important that the teacher is on hand to encourage, to listen to the on-going work and to provide help in a variety of ways. It is also important that the work is shared, that teachers monitor the work done – eg by tape recording – and that there is time for discussion about the various ideas that have been produced.

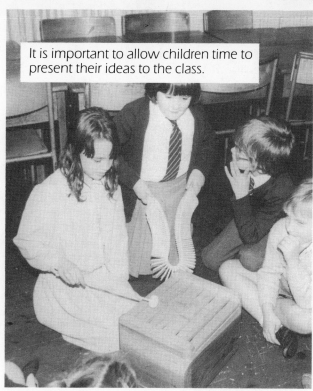

It is important to allow children time to present their ideas to the class.

Poems as a stimulus for drama work

Objectives

In developing an understanding and enjoyment of language children will enjoy poetry as much for its content as for its pleasurable sounds. Story or narrative verses appeal to children, in part because of their economic use of language. Children enjoy the pace at which they tell a story or relate to an incident. One way of interpreting and building in another dimension to these verses is to dramatise or mime them. This could be done using the complete poem to enact out a storyline such as 'The Owl and the Pussy Cat' – a nonsense poem by Edward Lear – or a more complex poem such as 'Legend' by Judith Wright (see page 182). Alternatively some ideas could be taken out and used as separate 'situations' to be worked on either as mime or conversation exercises.

The smile that grew

Once upon a sunbeam
A smile came tumbling down,
It landed 'plop' on Sarah's lips
And covered up her frown.

The frown was very angry
And shouted 'Go away!'
But Sarah said 'I like my smile,
I won't wear you today.'

She smiled at baby brother
And grinned at mum and dad,
She even smiled at Naughty Ned
Whose manners were so bad.

Baby stopped a-crying
Under Sarah's spell,
Mum and Dad stopped worrying
To spare a grin as well.

Naughty Ned stopped teasing
To offer her a choc,
Her smile delighted Sarah so,
She took it for a walk.

She smiled at two policemen
A-sternly walking by,
She beamed at Grumpy Grandpa
And winked a saucy eye.

She grinned at busy workmen
A-working up on high,
Her face was all a-twinkle
At shoppers passing by.

Level of development

Five- to eleven-year-olds.

Classroom organisation

Let the children absorb and enjoy the mood and the atmosphere created by the following two poems. Read them aloud and encourage the children to read them aloud. Use them as a basis for discussion about other things that make people smile/laugh. The children could then work in pairs or small groups to interpret some of the ideas in mime. Work on facial gestures is particularly important. Encourage them to reflect contrasting facial gestures. Children who may be inhibited about using their voices in front of others are often less inhibited about expressing themselves in mime and gestures.

She smiled at tired businessmen
A-running for their train,
And when surprised, they raised their hats
She beamed at them again.

She passed some foreign children,
She didn't have to speak,
A smile was all they needed
To give them all a treat.

Her look was so appealing
Between her hops and skips,
That little smiles began to grow
On other people's lips.

The smiles began to broaden
Till at the close of day,
Everyone was smiling
Though 'Why?' they couldn't say.

They followed Sarah home again
And gave a hearty cheer
For Sarah, who had made them smile,
Their frowns to disappear.

So Sarah got to thinking
Of what her smile had done,
She thought awhile 'I'll keep my smile,
So many friends I've won.'

She gazed down from her window
Her heart full to the brim,
'I didn't know my smile would grow,
The town is one big grin.'

Lilian Murray

Daddy fell into the pond

Everyone grumbled. The sky was gray.
We had nothing to do and nothing to say.
We were nearing the end of a dismal day,
And there seemed to be nothing beyond,
   THEN
  Daddy fell into the pond!

And everyone's face grew merry and bright,
And Timothy danced for sheer delight.
'Give me the camera, quick, oh quick!
He's crawling out of the duckweed.' Click!

Then the gardener suddenly slapped his knee,
And doubled up, shaking silently,
And the ducks all quacked as if they were daft
And it sounded as if the old drake laughed.

Oh, there wasn't a thing that didn't respond
   WHEN
  Daddy fell into the pond!
      Alfred Noyes

The Turnip is an amusing poem which may appeal to younger children because of its nonsensical content. It could work well with a group reciting the words and another group miming the 'story'. Encourage the children to really exaggerate the nonsense side of the verses and to 'build' their own ideas about the different characters: Mr Finney and his wife, Lizzie and Susie.

The turnip

Mr Finney had a turnip,
And it grew, and it grew,
And it grew behind the barn,
And the turnip did no harm.

And it grew, and it grew
Till it could grow no taller,
And Mr Finney took it
And he put it in the cellar.

There it lay, there it lay
Till it began to rot,
And his daughter Lizzie took it
And she put it in the pot.

And she boiled it, and she boiled it
As long as she was able,
And his daughter Susie took it
And she put it on the table.

Mr Finney and his wife
Both sat down to sup,
And they ate, and they ate,
And they ate the turnip up!
      Old Rhyme

Just Like Me and Rat-a-tat-tat are traditional rhymes with an element of nonsense. Rhymes like this can often encourage inhibited children – where the idea is just to say something, however silly, to keep the flow of dialogue. A useful 'game' to play for encouraging children to think quickly is 'Word associations' (see page 185).

Rat-a-tat-tat

Rat-a-tat-tat. Who is that?
Only grandma's pussy cat.
What do you want?
A pint of milk
Where's your money?
In my pocket
Where's your pocket?
I forgot it
Oh you silly pussy cat.
      Anonymous

Just like me

I went up one pair of stairs;
Just like me.
I went up two pairs of stairs;
Just like me.
I went into a room;
Just like me.
I looked out of a window;
Just like me.
And there I saw a monkey;
Just like me.
      Anonymous

Shy children are often less inhibited about expressing themselves in mime and gestures.

Resources

Faber Book of Nursery Verse Barbara Ireson (Ed), Faber & Faber

Now we are Six A A Milne, Methuen

When we were Young A A Milne, Methuen

Please tell me Pterodactyl: a book of monsterous verse Charles Connel, Hamlyn Group

Strictly Private compiled by Roger McGough, Kestrel Books

Story Chest (Sun smile; More, More, More; Taddalik) June Mesler, E J Arnold

How Strong the Roots: poems of exile compiled by Howard Sergeant, Bell & Hyman

Dread Beat and Blood Linton Kwesi Johnson, distributed by Bogle-L'Overture Publishers Ltd, 141 Coldershaw Road, London W13 9DU

The Adventures of Tom Bombadil J R R Tolkein, Allen and Unwim

Where's that Poem? An index of poems for children Helen Morris, Basil Blackwell

Wheel around the Word compiled by Chris Searle, Macdonald

A Packet of Poems: poems about food collected by Jill Bennett, Oxford University Press

Please Mrs Butler Allan Ahlberg, Viking Kestrel

Poetry 1 – Dragon's Smoke collected by Wes Magee, Basil Blackwell

Poetry 2 – A Shooting Star collected by Wes Magee, Basil Blackwell

Sky in the Pie Roger McGough, Kestrel Books

Hairy Tails and Nursery Crimes Michael Rosen, Andre Deutsch

Don't Put Mustard in the Custard Michael Rosen and Quentin Blake, Andre Deutsch

You Can't Catch Me Michael Rosen and Quentin Blake, Andre Deutsch

Wouldn't you Like to Know? Michael Rosen and Quentin Blake, Andre Deutsch

Everybody Here compiled by Michael Rosen, Bodley Head

But still I love her just the same Angela Sommer-Bodenburg, Burke

Poems that go bump in the night Ian and Zenka Woodward, Beaver Books

Oxford Book of Poetry for Children compiled by Edward Blishen, Oxford University Press

I Din Do Nuttin and Other Poems John Agard, Magnet

The Kingfisher Book of Children's Poetry compied by Michael Rosen, Kingfisher Books

Season Songs Ted Hughes, Faber (includes 'Golden boy' referred to on page 185).

Indexes

Title index

Note: the first line of the poem or rhyme has been used for untitled works.

T

U

V

W

Y

First line index

Skills index

A

Accompanying (on an instrument), 117, 152, 171
Action rhymes, chants and stories, 1–35
Acting out, 24, 53, 192
Adding (maths), 41, 54
Adult supervision (playground games), 64, 66
Answering (see Response)

B

Beat
    accenting (stressing), 118, 125
    keeping (marking), 6, 12, 19, 20, 24, 27, 117, 118, 119, 125, 130–133, 140–144, 147, 149, 152, 171, 185
    silent (see Gaps)
Beats, grouping, 117, 125
Bumps (skipping), 68

C

Chanting, 23, 25
Circling, 18, 82, 83, 84, 85, 86, 158
Clapping, 11, 12, 19, 20, 24, 27, 48, 75, 76, 117, 118, 119, 122, 128, 130–132, 134, 136, 137, 140, 143, 144, 171, 185, 186
Climate, 68
Colours, 66, 67
Co-ordination, 4, 6, 7, 21, 23, 72, 131, 170
    of language and movement, 3, 115–116
Confidence, 7, 34
Conservation of number, 41
Copying, 122, 151, 153, 156
Corporate activity (see Group participation)
Counting, 40, 53, 117, 165, 170
Creating (see Inventing)
Creating images, 186

D

Dancing, 17, 19, 20, 29, 31, 82, 116, 117, 122, 125, 128, 136, 145, 153, 154, 156, 158, 160, 164, 171
Dipping (selection), 102
Discriminating aurally, 147
Do-si-do (dance), 171
Drama, 30, 144

Dramatising, 17, 19, 28, 32, 127, 192
Drawing, 45, 52, 54, 78, 81
Dynamics (see Loud/quiet)

E

Echoing, 122, 127, 151
Experimenting, 4, 10, 164, 189
Exploring sounds, 139, 189

F

Fast/slow, 120, 142, 143, 149
Faster/slower, 142, 143, 149
Following (words), 53

G

Gallopsies (skipping), 72
Gaps (in the beat), 4, 14, 118, 134, 185, 186
Gestures, facial, 18, 192
Graphical work, 57
Group participation, 7, 18, 38, 65
Guessing, 185

H

Haiku, 185
Hopping, 5, 13, 143, 145

I

Identifying (odds and evens), 58
Illustrating, 46, 53
Imitating, 16, 19
Improvising, 29, 119
Informal game traditions, 65
Internalising (beat and melody), 21, 133
Inventing, 10, 11, 14, 15, 17, 28, 29, 57, 67, 99, 107, 122, 124, 128, 145

J

Jumping, 6, 68, 69, 74, 85, 149, 161
    in and out, 72, 74

K

Keeping the beat or pulse (see Beat)

Topic index

Action rhymes

Action story songs

Animals

Ball games

Chants and songs

Circle and group games

Clapping games

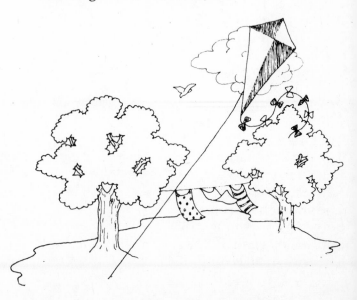

Weather

Acknowledgements

The publishers would like to thank the pupils and staff of the following schools for allowing us to photograph them at work for inclusion in this Handbook: Wykeham Infant School, Hornchurch; Canonbury Infant School, London; Lakey Lane Primary School, Birmingham; Edgewick Infant and Junior School, Coventry. The publishers also gratefully acknowledge the preparation of artwork for inclusion in the Handbook by pupils at Coten End Middle School, Warwick.

A particular thank you is given to Layla, Hannah, Ella and Gaia for their help in compiling the chapters on Playground games and Nonsense rhymes and games.

The publishers gratefully acknowledge permission from the following sources to reproduce copyrighted material: Kelman Music Corporation for 'I'm a little teapot'; Century Hutchinson Ltd for 'Would you dare?' and 'Look at your hat' from *Over and Over Again* B Ireson and C Rowe (Beaver Books);
Belwin Mills Music Ltd for 'The dingle dangle scarecrow' adapted from *Wide Awake* by M Russell-Smith and G Russell-Smith; Harrap Ltd and Columbia Pictures for 'I wiggle my fingers' and 'Ten miles from home' from *Singing Fun* L Wood and L Scott; E J Arnold and Son Ltd for 'Loud and soft' by K Todd and 'Everyone can clap hands' from *Poetry Corner* ed Sylvia Mary Leach; Bowmer Publishing Company for 'I can wiggle my fingers' and 'Jack in the box' from *Music: a way of life for the young child* K Baylis and M E Ramsey (Mosby); Pitman Publishing Ltd, London for 'Ten merry men' from *Number Rhymes and Finger Plays* E R Boyle and K Bartlett; Silver, Burdett & Ginn for 'Five little spacemen' adapted from *Singing and Rhyming* of Our Singing World series © 1959, 1957, 1950; Hamlyn Publishing for 'Dinosaur' by Charles Connell from *Please Tell me Pterodactyl*; A & C Black for 'Two cats' by Samuel Marshak from *Nonsense Rhymes* ed Peggy Blakeley, 'Farmer Jackson's farm' by Clive Sanson from *Counting Rhymes*, 'Miss Mary Mac', 'There was a princess long ago' and 'The wheels on the bus' from *Okki-tokki-unga*, and 'Bird in a cage' from *Folk Songs from the East*, compiled by Janet Tobbitt; Penguin Books Ltd for 'There's a red brick wall' from *Stickleback, Stickleback and Other Minnow Rhymes* (Kestrel Books, 1977) © Nancy Chambers, 'Who's that?' by James Kirkup from *Round About Nine* (Frederick Warne), 'Sudden shower' by Yosa Buson from *Penguin Book of Japanese Verse* translated by Geoffrey Bownas and Anthony Thwaite (The Penguin Poets, 1964) © Geoffrey Bownas and Anthony Thwaite, 1964;
Oxford University Press for 'Snow' by boy aged 8, 'Pearls on the grass' by Geeta Mohanty and 'The railway station' by Gwyneth from Wordscapes ed Barry Maybury © Oxford University Press, 1970 and 'Reflections' by Wendy Maggs and 'He is a sad dragon' by Mark from *Thoughtscapes* ed Barry Maybury © Oxford University Press, 1972;
Simon & Schuster Inc for 'Bingo was his name oh' by Marie Winn and Alan Miller from *The Fireside Book of Children's Songs* © 1966;
Faber and Faber Ltd for 'Night mail' by W H Auden from *Collected Poems*;
Angus & Robertson (UK) Ltd for 'Legend' by Judith Wright from *Collected Poems* 1942–1970 © Judith Wright 1971;
Spike Milligan Productions Ltd for 'A baby sardine' by Spike Milligan from *Silly Verse for Kids*;
Atheneum Publishers for 'In the sun' from *I Feel the Same Way* © Lillian Moore;
Doubleday & Company Inc for 'Spring rain' by Matzuo Basho from *Introduction to Haiku* Harold G Henderson © 1958 by Harold G Henderson;
Blackwood, Pillans and Wilson for 'Daddy fell into the pond' from *Daddy Fell into the Pond and Other Poems*;
David Higham Associates Ltd for 'The tide in the river' by Eleanor Farjeon from *Silver*

Sand and Snow (Michael Joseph);
Charles Scribner's Sons for 'August afternoon' from *Open the Door* Marion Edey and Dorothy Grider © Marion Edey and Dorothy Grider. Copyright under the Berne Convention;
David Evans for 'The rocket' and the additional verses for 'Tidey oh' from *Sing a Song One* (Thomas Nelson & Sons Ltd);
Mrs Wyn David Evans and Penguin Books Ltd for 'Galloping horses' from *This Little Puffin*;
Barbara Ireson for 'The grocers' from *Rhyme Time* (Beaver Books);
Neil Adams for 'The song the train sang' from *Travelling Light*;
The Society of Authors on behalf of the copyright owner, Mrs Iris Wise for 'And it was windy weather' by James Stephens;
Tin Pan Alley Music Ltd for the words for 'English country garden';
'Pass the Pebble on', English words by Shirley Winfield, Music Centre ILEA, original words Felix Cobbson.
Judith Nichols and *Junior Education* for 'It's two weeks old' and 'I live in the summer';
Sandy Brownjohn and *Junior Education Special* 'The moon's a great big ball', 'A big white light bulb', 'A scream of fear', 'The press' and 'The dream';
Elizabeth Chapman and *Junior Education Special* for 'Presents big and small', 'Falling on the ground' and 'Shepherds and wise men'.

The following poems which were specially written for this Handbook are © Leonora T Davies; 'Look at the fish', 'I'm a great big lorry', 'How did Ben/Jane come to school', 'Put on your shoes', and 'I can hear two people'.

Every effort has been made to trace and acknowledge contributions. If any right has been omitted the publishers offer their apologies and will rectify this in subsequent editions following notification.

Other Scholastic books

Bright Ideas titles

Previous titles in this series available are:

Bright Ideas Seasonal Activities
0 590 70831 7   £5.45

Bright Ideas Language Development
0 590 70834 1   £5.45

Bright Ideas Science
0 590 70833 3   £5.45

Bright Ideas Christmas Art and Craft
0 590 70832 5   £5.45

Bright Ideas Reading Activities
0 590 70535 0   £5.45

Bright Ideas Maths Activities
0 590 70534 2   £5.45

Teacher Handbooks titles

Titles in this series available are:

Teacher Handbooks Reading
0 590 70691 8   £7.95

Teacher Handbooks Language Resources
0 590 70692 6   £7.95

Teacher Handbooks Putting on a Performance
0 590 70801 5   £7.95

Teacher Handbooks Maths
0 590 70800 7   £7.95

More Bright Ideas Christmas Art and Craft
0 590 70601 2   £5.45

Bright Ideas Classroom Management
0 590 70602 0   £5.45

Bright Ideas Games for PE
0 590 70690 X   £5.45

Bright Ideas Crafty Moneymakers
0 590 70689 6   £5.45

Bright Ideas Music
0 590 70700 0   £5.45

Bright Ideas Assemblies
0 590 70693 4   £5.45

Bright Ideas Writing
0 590 70701 9   £5.45

Bright Ideas Lifesavers
0 590 70694 2   £5.45

Bright Ideas Christmas Activities
0 590 70803 1   £5.45

Bright Ideas Spelling
0 590 70802 3   £5.45

Bright Ideas History
0 590 70804 X   £5.45

Set of any six titles £27

Write to Scholastic Publications Ltd, Westfield Road, Southam, Leamington Spa, Warwickshire CV33 0JH. Enclose your remittance. Make cheques payable to Scholastic Publications Ltd.